Proofreading Practice

Ralph Ruby, Jr.

J. Weston Walch, Publisher
Portland, Maine

Certified Chain of Custody
Promoting Sustainable
Forest Management
www.sfiprogram.org

SGS-SFI/COC-US09/5501

1   2   3   4   5   6   7   8   9   10

ISBN 0–8251–1604–X

Copyright © 1989
J. Weston Walch, Publisher
P.O. Box 658 • Portland, Maine 04104-0658

Printed in the United States of America

Contents

General Errors

Review

Introduction

In considering all types of communication for today's society, the following important question still remains: Does your correspondence show careful preparation and proofreading?

Proofreading Practice is designed to help students become better at the art of proofreading. The material is divided into six sections. Section I consists of proofreader marks and is subdivided into six categories: paragraphing, spacing, size, punctuation, position, and insertion and deletion. Section II presents, in brief form, the rules of English that will be used, when applicable, throughout this set. Section III is concerned with punctuation errors and contains individual documents dealing with such problem areas as the comma, the exclamation point, the dash, the colon, and others. Section IV deals with capitalization errors and contains individual exercises that stress such problem areas as the salutation and complimentary closing, a phrase or sentence following a colon, the first word of every section of an outline, and others. Section V is concerned with general errors such as spelling, numerical, and typographical. Section VI is a review section that deals with several communication documents, each containing a variety of errors.

The following references were consulted during the preparation of this set: *Hodges' Harbrace College Handbook, English on the Job, English Grammar and Composition,* and *Business Communications—Principles and Methods.*

This set of proofreading materials was designed to: (1) acquaint students with proofreader marks and how to use them, (2) provide hands-on material for students after the introduction of specific English rules, and (3) review English rules and proofreading procedures.

I suggest that you introduce the proofreader marks and rules of English presented on the first four copy masters. Then review the rules of English and specific proofreader marks for each exercise as it is introduced. These are noted for each master in the next section, Teacher Guide and Answers. This will reinforce the student's knowledge of the English rules and marks. The exercises were designed to be flexible and may be used in the individual instructor's order of preference. For this reason instructors may wish to try different strategies when using the exercises contained in this set. For example, Business Education Typewriting instructors may wish to have their students type a correct copy.

On a rare occasion the stated English rule in this set may be challenged, which is why specific references are mentioned above. If a legitimate challenge is raised, please refer to the reference(s) used in your classroom for an interpretation.

Any question regarding this set should be directed to Dr. Ralph Ruby, Jr., c/o J. Weston Walch, Publisher, Box 658, Portland, Maine, 04104.

Teacher Guide and Answers

5. Punctuation

> RULE: Use an <u>apostrophe:</u>
> A. for contractions
> B. to indicate the possessive form of nouns
> C. to indicate the plural form of words referred to as words

FUTURE BUSINESS LEADERS OF AMERICA
MANN HIGH SCHOOL
Agenda for Meeting, May 1, 19--
Mann High School Library, 4:00 P.M.

1. Call to Order	Jerry Abbott
2. Roll Call	Don Bramlett
3. Minutes of April Meeting	Don Bramlett
4. Report of Officers	
B a. Treasurer's	Gary Lunsford
B b. Vice President's	Albert Cressman
5. New Business	Jerry Abbott

     a. Election of new delegates is scheduled for our next meeting.

B, B, A
     b. The state test results from last year indicate that our chapter was weak spelling proper possessive plurals. Ex: men's—ladies'. Also it's
C
     important to avoid too many *and*'s in the written communications test.

6. Adjournment	Jerry Abbott

6. Punctuation

> RULE: Use a <u>colon</u> after:
> A. an introductory clause that introduces an enlargement of the meaning expressed in the introductory clause
> B. each of the introductory words in the heading of a memo
> C. an introductory statement containing the word *following*

B   TO⊙ Distributors

                FROM: Consumer Products Division

                DATE: March 18, 19--

B   SUBJECT⊙ Promotion

C   The following items are important points for consideration⊙

         Job progress lies in one direction: Thorough training and the ability to adapt to ever-changing needs will invariably encourage advancement.

         You are in a powerful role: You represent a multimillion-dollar company that is the leader in the field of home-care products.

A   We offer eighty-three products under eight general care areas⊙ Personal, Furniture, Floor, Rug and Carpet, General Home, Odor Control, Insect Control, and Car.

         Note that we plan to open three new areas in the next year: Laundry Care, Wall and Ceiling Care, and Basement Playroom Care.

A   Distributors must have a complete knowledge of all products⊙ Classes to demonstrate and learn about new products will meet monthly.

C   The following will increase your regular sales⊙ Complete knowledge of all products, completion of the sales promotion seminar program, and, of course, hard work and dedication.

A   The goal of becoming a gold-level distributor lies ahead⊙ Mastering the product line, determination, and our strong leadership can assure your place among the select.

         BP

7. Punctuation

> **RULE:** Use a <u>comma</u>:
> A. to separate city and state in an address
> B. to separate the day from the year
> C. after the complimentary closing when using mixed punctuation
> D. to separate numbers of four or more digits
> E. to set off phrases in apposition
> F. to separate a dependent clause at the beginning of a sentence
> G. to set off introductory and transition words
> H. for clarity

ELCO FUEL OIL COMPANY	Telephone	DAYS	212 555-2314
1002 Energy Lane		NIGHTS	212 555-2333
Satsop, WA		EMERGENCY	212 555-2222

COAL ● COMMERCIAL OIL ● HOME HEATING OIL ● KEROSENE

B   August 9, 19--

Mr. Charles K. Bruce
Ideal Toy Company
49 Harding Avenue
A   Satsop, WA 98583

Dear Mr. Bruce:

D You are correct in estimating that you use over 9,000 gallons of No. 2 fuel oil each year to
H heat your building. The cost is high, we agree.

Perhaps you should consider converting to No. 5 fuel oil and a Duncan Heavy-Oil Burner.
F, G By so doing, you could save up to 7 cents on each gallon. Actually, though the heavier oil
E, G costs less per gallon than the lighter oil, it gives 15% more heat. Furthermore, the Duncan
D Burner is efficient and dependable. Last year over 10,000 burners were converted to take
advantage of the savings.

The enclosed circular shows the yearly savings on some typical installations that we have
F recently converted. If you are interested, we shall be glad to show you any of these
installations and to arrange a meeting with the satisfied purchaser.

C Sincerely,

Edward J. Warren
Sales Manager

FD

Enclosure

8. Punctuation

RULE: Use a <u>dash</u>:
    A. prior to a summarizing statement
    B. to set off an independent interpolation that is a clause
    C. to set off a long appositive

PARKHILL SAVINGS BANK
1372 Rollins Drive
Springfield, VT 05156
Telephone 555 333-9009

June 15, 19--

Mr. Thomas Raynor
264 Brandon Street
Springfield, VT 05156

Dear Mr. Raynor:

Permit me to extend a friendly greeting to you as a member of our large family of depositors. We appreciate your patronage and trust that you will make use of the various services that the Parkhill Savings Bank offers.

C I wish particularly to bring to your attention one of our newer facilities—"over-the-counter" SAVINGS BANK LIFE INSURANCE. Few people are aware that life insurance can be coupled with a long-range savings account. **B** This type of insurance—believe it **B** or not—provides unusual policy benefits, yet the net cost is low because no selling commissions are paid.

On your next visit to our bank, why not make inquiry at the Life Insurance desk about the type of insurance best suited to your needs? We don't want you—or any of our **A** customers—to lose your home, your land holdings, your personal investments—all your **A** lifetime acquirements—because of negligence on our part. I am sure you will be pleasantly surprised to learn of the many advantages of SAVINGS BANK INSURANCE.

Please accept my cordial good wishes. We shall look forward to serving you for a long time to come.

Sincerely yours,

Howard Dunnigan
President

WO

9. Punctuation

> **RULE:** Use a <u>diagonal line</u>:
>   **A.** to indicate the end of a line when quoting poetry
>   **B.** when typing certain abbreviations

—————————— **MEMO** ——————————

TO: All Employees

FROM: Fred Simpson, President

DATE: January 26, 19--

SUBJECT: Correspondence

A, A, A In dating future correspondence, please remember the following; "Thirty days hath September,/April, June, and November,/February hath twenty-eight alone,/And all the rest have thirty-one."

B All mail for Howard Brown should be sent to John Johnson, c/o Station WCBQ, Independence, IA.

JT

10. Punctuation

RULE: Use a <u>exclamation point</u>:
      A. after an interjection and the complete sentence when both are exclamatory
      B. to express strong emotion

BIG 10 STORES
Bald Knob, Jonesboro, Newburgh, Walden, and Warwick

CUSTOMER'S NAME
STREET ADDRESS
CITY, STATE ZIP CODE

Dear LAST NAME:

      To help FIRNAME get the most out of HIS/HER money we are having a special "Products Give-A-Way" on Thursday evening, October 16th. Oh, what bargains are in
A store for you(!)Every item in the store will be specially marked, and certain items will be
B red-tagged for Super Savings(!)Enclosed you will find five coupons that you may use to
B receive additional savings on any item you choose. Save those coupons(!)You won't want to miss a single opportunity to increase your shopping value and further your savings.

      In order to prepare ourselves for this spectacular event, we will be closed from 1:00 to 6:00 P.M. on October 15. If you have any questions about the event, don't hesitate to call. Our switchboard operators will be prepared to answer any and all inquiries.

      We are looking forward to the pleasure of your presence at our "Products Give-A-
B Way." Don't forget October 16, and don't forget your coupons(!)
B See you there(!)

MANAGER'S NAME
Store Manager

SERVING OUR CUSTOMERS BETTER

NOTE TO INSTRUCTOR—This is to be a merge letter. Items in capitals would be replaced with specific data from a data base.

11. Punctuation

RULE: Use a <u>hyphen</u>:
  A. to indicate a division of a word at the end of a line
  B. to show the omission of the word *to*
  C. to suspend the first part of a hyphenated compound
  D. in compounds containing prepositions

TO: All Personnel

FROM: President Howell

DATE: May 8, 19--

SUBJECT: Board of Directors Meeting--May 25, 19--

B
D
Plans are being made for the Board of Directors meeting to be held the end of this month (May 25, 19-2). Ex-president Whitlow will be in attendance to help facilitate preparation for the change-in-policy statements. All chairpersons of the departments involved need to get their reports into my office on Monday.

C, C, C
C, A
C
We will be discussing short- and long-term contracts; some additional benefits for two-, three-, and four-member households; the possibility of a once- or twice-monthly bulletin to de-partments with vital news and information; complaints that have been turned in to the vice president's office; and the formation of a three- or five-member buffer team to improve relations between the working staff and the president's office.

Please have your input for the above items of discussion ready and turned in to the vice president's office by the 1st also.

Thank you.

DFW

12. Punctuation

RULE: Use <u>parentheses</u> to:
    A. set off a group of words having no definite bearing on the main thought
    B. enclose dates indicating a period of time
    C. enclose numbers expressed in figures for clarification

---

BUYING A HOME

How to Assess Your Housing Needs

A   More than 64% of all American families own their homes, and the percentage is growing. (See figs. 1 and 2.) Perhaps your family is planning to become involved in what will possibly be its largest purchase ever.

B   Owning a home gives many people a sense of security. During the Browning era (1785-1880) it was established that homeowners take great pride in ownership and find satisfaction in maintaining their property. Buying a home is often regarded as one of the soundest investments a family can make.

Disadvantages should also be carefully considered before taking the big step. It is more difficult to move when you own than when you rent. Home ownership entails financial risk as well as extra work and expense. In addition to the substantial drain on savings resulting from the purchase, maintenance costs must be taken into account.

C   Which is best for your family—to buy or rent? Weigh the pro and cons so that your decision does not verge on impulse. For further information and advice, send us twenty-five ($25) dollars with your name and address and we will be delighted to set up a consultation for you with our lawyers.

Better Homes Bureau

13. Punctuation

RULE: Use a **period**:
A. at the end of a complete sentence
B. after an abbreviation

ITINERARY OF BILL HUTCHINSON
March 18 to 21
Atlanta to Miami

MONDAY, MARCH 18, ATLANTA

9:15 AM   Depart Birmingham on Pan Am, Flight 142.

B
A   10:00 AM   Arrive at Atlanta. Meet with Frank Deloach to discuss contract terms for Clark Co. at the Airport Restaurant. Frank will drive you to Stouffer's Inn, where your room is reserved.

B   3:00 PM   Meet with Garry George to discuss possibilities of production expansion at the Vans Co. Atlanta branch.

TUESDAY, MARCH 19, ATLANTA TO GAINESVILLE

A   8:35 AM   Depart Atlanta on TWA, Flight 35.

A
B   10:30 AM   Arrive at Gainesville. Reservations for rental car have been made with Avis. Drive to Evans Inc. Gainesville branch, to meet with plant manager, Kenneth Bentley.

WEDNESDAY, MARCH 20, GAINESVILLE TO MIAMI

9:00 AM   Depart Gainesville on Delta, Flight 751.

A   10:35 AM   Arrive at Miami. Reservations for room have been made with Hilton Fountainebleu. Rent car at the airport.

B   1:00 PM   Meet with Ray Hall to discuss possibilities of opening Pool and Spa Ltd. branch in Miami.

THURSDAY, MARCH 21, MIAMI TO BIRMINGHAM

A   8:35 AM   Depart Miami on Delta, Flight 101.

11:00 AM   Connect in Atlanta, Delta, Flight 49.

1:20 PM   Arrive in Birmingham.

NOTE TO INSTRUCTOR—Mention to students that the correct form within text for times of day is A.M. and P.M., not AM and PM.

14. Punctuation

> RULE: Use a <u>question mark</u>:
>   A. after a direct question

DEATSMAN & MARTIN, INC.   Telephone 333 555-8712
9685 Melody Lane
Venus, PA 16364 _____

December 20, 19--

Mrs. Frank S. Johnson
19 Wayne Street
Venus, PA 16364

Dear Mrs. Johnson:

A Have you often wondered if your child would enjoy learning to play the piano? Have you
A hesitated to do anything about it, however, because you thought it would be too expensive?
If so, you will surely be interested in learning about our unusual offer.

We will lend you a new piano for two weeks with no obligation on your part. The piano will
be delivered to your home, and we will provide a qualified teacher who will give your child
two piano lessons absolutely free.

If you would prefer a longer trial period, you may select a piano on a rental basis, and we
will provide 12 free lessons for your child. The entire amount paid as a rental fee will be
applied to the selling price should you decide to purchase the piano at the end of the trial
period.

We invite you to visit our Music Department to discuss the many advantages of this offer.
You will then have an opportunity to see and hear a selection of pianos from the world's
A most renowned piano manufacturers. Sound interesting? Call immediately for an
appointment.

Sincerely,

Jerome Q. Hayes, Manager
Music Department

VSD

15. Punctuation

RULE: Use <u>quotation marks</u> to enclose:
    A. words used in a special sense
    B. technical words
    C. titles of articles

ACID RAIN—A TIME BOMB

B, B   The term "acid rain," coined by Angus Smith, a 19th-century Scottish scientist, has become the environmental problem of the 80s.

George Handley of Bookhaven Institute, who has conducted studies around the world, reports that atmospheric sulfur concentrations are a problem in the entire Northern Hemisphere and parts of the Southern Hemisphere.

The problem seems especially bad in America's Northeast. Industries and utilities in the Midwest spew sulfur dioxide and oxides of nitrogen into the troposphere, where they enter the jet stream and travel eastward. These sulfate and nitrate particles combine with water during any form of precipitation to form sulfuric and nitric acids.

Ohio produces 9,000 tons of sulfur dioxide daily. This amounts to twice the total output of the six New England states, New York, and New Jersey combined.

A, A   The Adirondacks, where already over 250 lakes are "dead" (devoid of fish life due to acidity), have acid levels that measured 3.54 pH, which is equivalent to the juice of a dill pickle.

The area from the Catskill Mountains to the Atlantic Ocean has been experiencing increased acidity levels despite local control of pollutants. In addition to water contamination of lake and streams, other problems have surfaced.

A, A   Some of our most beloved landmarks, such as the Statue of Liberty, are being eroded by the "rains." Stone buildings like the Metropolitan Museum may need a total facelift every five years if the acid level in the precipitation remains as high as it is now.

A, A   Other studies in southern New York State show that the "rain" is wearing away the natural waxy coating on leaves of most plants, leaving them more susceptible to fungus diseases. Once again modern humanity has created a monster, and humanity must now come up with solutions to combat this problem.

C, C   For additional information, read the article "Producing Acid Rain" by Thomas Dew in the latest issue of the *Journal of Forestry*.

16. Punctuation

RULE: Use a <u>semicolon</u>:
    A. between series of lengthy phrases

FALLS ELECTRICAL COMPANY
45 BROADWAY
LOS ALAMOS, NM 87544
         Telephone 333 555-0092

June 7, 19--

The Buffalo Record
82 Niagara Street
Los Alamos, NM 87544

Attention: Advertising Department

Gentlemen:

Kindly place the following advertisements in the Classified Advertisements Supplement of your paper on Sunday, June 23. The articles are to be placed in the HELP WANTED section.

A, A   STENOGRAPHER-TYPIST, able to take rapid dictation and do general office work, starting salary, $235, permanent position and good chance for advancement; experience not essential, but must be willing and easily
A   adaptable, reply with complete qualifications. Box . . ., RECORD

A, A, A   INDIVIDUAL, high school graduate, knowledge of typing, shorthand, and Spanish, export dept, experience unnecessary; $1,355 a month, reply with complete details. Box . . ., RECORD

Please assign individual "Box Numbers" to each of these inserts and send this information to us. You will, of course, charge these insertions to our account.

Sincerely,

Eugene Fischer
Personnel Director

EN

17. Punctuation

> RULE: Use an <u>underscore</u>:
>   A. for <u>emphasis</u>

PARKHILL SAVINGS BANK

A Guide to Our Services

1. <u>Insured Savings.</u> Individual accounts insured by Federal Deposit Insurance Corporation up to $100,000; joint accounts up to $200,000.

2. <u>Banking by Mail.</u> The easy way to save regularly. Safe, convenient, timesaving.

A 3. <u>Mortgage Loans.</u> F.H.A. insured. Long terms, easy payments.

A 4. <u>Savings Bank Money Orders.</u> Cost, only $2.00 each for any amount up to $1,000.

5. <u>Safe-Deposit Boxes.</u> Yearly rental, $9.50 and up (plus tax).

6. <u>Traveler's Checks.</u> Protection for your funds while you travel.

A 7. <u>Christmas Club.</u> For Christmas and other year-end expenses. Deposits of $.50 weekly and up accepted.

A 8. <u>Savings Bank Life Insurance.</u> Full protection at low cost. Liberal dividends. All types of policies available.

A 9. <u>Foreign Remittances.</u> Reasonable rates on money orders, checks, radio, cable.

18. Capitalization

> RULE: <u>Capitalize</u> the first word:
>   A. of every sentence

PLAY REVIEW

A   Last night I saw an exciting new play entitled *It's in the Wind.* Never before have I seen such an engaging performance by a newcomer to the stage as I did last night. It was

A   brief; but, oh yes, I'll never forget it. Susan Greer (don't forget that name) is a natural. My theatre partner said, "She makes me want to just hold her in my arms and protect her from

A   all the injustices that are sure to come her way." I agreed and then I heard someone sitting

A   behind me say, "Don't you feel sorry for the rest of the cast? They can't compare their performance with Susan's." So I feel compelled to say something about the rest of the cast. They were marvelous. If they hadn't been, then Susan's presentation of the lead would

A   have surely fallen short without the support from the rest of the players. For one to come away from a play so thoroughly enjoyable and hear fellow members of the audience say, "I'm coming back as soon as I can get a seat," you have to realize the entire cast was superb.

A   What else can I say? Oh, what a performance! Don't miss it!

19. Capitalization

RULE: Capitalize the first word:
B. of every direct quotation

DORIGHT CORPORATION, LTD.
212 High Street
Westfield, MA 01085
333 555-4441

April 24, 19--

Mr. Vito White
27 Paddock Place
Westfield, MA 01085

Dear Mr. White:

B   When did you last tell your staff, "Things have to improve around here or some heads will roll"? Are you always forced to be on top of things at the office when you would rather be out in the community furthering your "community relations"?

B, B   If you answered "Never" or "No" to the questions above, then you may not need our
B, B   services, but if you answered "Occasionally" or "Yes," then we feel sure you need us. We have made a survey that we think you will be interested in. It includes the problems mentioned in addition to many other business entanglements.

B   You are now asking, "What must I do to take advantage of this offer?" Simply send us a short letter stating your needs, and we will forward you all the information we have that even remotely concerns your problem area.

Thank you for your interest.

Sincerely,

Jonathan Doright
President

LD

20. Capitalization

RULE: Capitalize the first word:
C. of an independent question within a sentence

STUDENTS, NOW HEAR THIS!

C   Are you often faced with the question, When am I going to get this term paper
C   finished? Or have you ever asked yourself, How will I ever get the answers to these
questions with the class load I have?

Many of you have a pretty full day—would you believe one study hall a week? Often
you find you've used your last study hall and that library assignment is due tomorrow. The
library doesn't close at the end of the eighth period; you can stay until 4:30 and take the
academic bus home.

Some materials you will need for research may not be taken from the library during
the school day, but they may be signed out at the close of school for overnight. Both general
and special encyclopedias as well as the reserve book collection are in this category. So
don't stand around complaining. Come on in and get busy. There is no reason you should
C   ask, Where is the opportunity I need to get ahead? We're always here.

In addition to fiction, nonfiction, and the familiar biographies, you will find reference books such as atlases, almanacs, dictionaries, thesauri, and secretarial handbooks. We
also have books of quotations and books on music, art, and etiquette.

Your library has more than just books. Don't forget periodicals, which may be signed
out for a period of two weeks. You may wish to consult the vertical file when doing research
work on facts not in book form such as maps, paintings, and art reproductions. Use the
record collection, the transparencies, and the filmstrips.

C   If you aren't sure about a book, just ask us questions such as, What is a thesaurus and
how can it help me? We are here just to answer such questions and to help you use all the
library facilities to their fullest.

Never hesitate to ask us for help!

The Librarians

READ   FOR   KNOWLEDGE

21. Capitalization

RULE: Capitalize the first word of a phrase or sentence following a colon when:
D1. the subject matter is formal
D2. the following material is a direct quotation

AMERICAN SAFE DRIVING COUNCIL   **TELEPHONE 333 555-1001**
BOX 458
NEW YORK, NY 10021

August 19, 19--

Mr. James H. Wetherell, Principal
Susquehanna High School
Susquehanna, PA 18847

Dear Mr. Wetherell:

You undoubtedly share the concern of responsible citizens over the fact that carelessness on the highways annually results in many deaths. Last year 41,000 people in the United States lost their lives as the direct result of automobile accidents. As our Highway

D2 Commissioner has often said: "We must have a continuing campaign for safe driving on our nation's highways."

Although drivers under age twenty-five represent 15% of all drivers, they account for 25% of the accidents. We would like to enlist your support in the promotion of safe driving among your high school students.

D1 Our program consists of promoting an awareness of: Automobile accident statistics, the importance of having a safe vehicle, and the importance of being a safe driver.

We can provide each student in your school with a copy of the enclosed brochure. If you would like to have one of our safe driving instructors put on a demonstration at your school, please write us.

D1 We hope your school will soon share our motto: Be smart, be sure, be safe.

Sincerely,

Oliver H. Seager
Director

EP

Enclosure

Note: An early response will assure you of a greater opportunity of scheduling on the date of your choice.

22. Capitalization

> RULE: <u>Capitalize</u> the first word:
>   E. and all nouns in the salutation
>   F. and all nouns in the complimentary closing

September 14, 19--

Mr. Harry Gelatt
President
Rotary Club of Chugwater
143 Main Street
Chugwater, WY 82210

E, E, E   Dear Mr. Gellatt:

We have embarked on a campaign to reduce the number of deaths occurring each year as a result of automobile accidents. We are seeking the support of local service organizations in publicizing the factors that contribute to the tragic traffic picture.

Our Speakers' Bureau is devoting its entire attention this year to traffic safety. Each speaker is prepared to present an illustrated lecture stressing the principal causes of traffic fatalities. Among the points discussed are: city traffic, driving on expressways, stopping distances, and holiday driving. The talk will emphasize the precautions drivers should observe to protect their own lives and the lives of others.

After you read the enclosed publicity release, we feel sure you will want to hear one of our speakers.

F   Sincerely yours,

Oliver H. Seager
Director

KR

Enclosure

DRIVE SMART --------------------------- DON'T BE A DUMMY

23. Capitalization

RULE: Capitalize the first word:
   G. in every section of an outline

GUIDES FOR SAFE DRIVING

Do you want to be a good driver? If you do, you will want to practice the following safe driving techniques:

Don't:

1. Drive with a dirty windshield or one cluttered with stickers.
2. Drive when you are sleepy, angry, or depressed.

G 3. Pass on curves or hills.

G 4. Allow too many people to get in your car.

G 5. "Tailgate."

6. Be a "show-off" while driving a car.
7. Cut in too soon after passing another car.
8. Drive after having an alcoholic drink.

Do:

1. Drive at lower speeds on slippery highways, in heavy traffic, and in bad weather.
2. Have good lights and dim them when traffic approaches.

G 3. Pay attention to stop signs, highway signs, or danger signs.

4. Have your brakes checked regularly.
5. Signal before you start, pass, stop, or back up.

G 6. Keep your mind on your driving, your eyes on the road, and your hands on the steering wheel.

G 7. Have good tires on all wheels.

8. Be a courteous driver!

24. Capitalization

RULE: <u>Capitalize</u> the names of:
      A. associations

A, A

The Community Council
Box 54621
Davenport, ND 58021

333 555-9009

February 10, 19--

Mr. & Mrs. Walter Morgan
67 Oak Street
Davenport, ND 58021

Dear Citizens:

A, A, A, A, A   Your Community Council has invited the American Red Cross to send a speaker to our July Open Meeting.

     The local chapter has graciously offered to send us a field representative who will talk about some of the work in which the Red Cross is most interested at the present time.

A, A   Although we have general information about the excellent work this organization is doing, it should be most interesting and valuable to hear first-hand details from a worker just returned from an actual combat zone.

     The meeting will be held at the Hotel Sampson at Main and Tenth streets.

     Will you make a special effort to be there promptly at 8:00 P.M. on Thursday, July 6?

Sincerely,

Henry S. Blake
Chairman

DH

25. Capitalization

RULE: Capitalize the names of:
     B. astronomical bodies

February 22, 19--

Amos R. Libra
2516 Legal Circle
Carson City, CA 89701

Dear Fellow Libra:

Have you ever taken advantage of the services offered by the Astrological Society to which you belong? Have you let them give you a complete "astrological check-up" to determine if

B, B, B
your future includes an alignment with Mars or if you will get caught up in the Milky Way and have a hard time relating to others in the galaxy?

We are now offering to you a special once-a-year deal where we can keep you informed of the year's events and the chances of Libra running into trouble with Serpens, the Snake. Your horoscope could be on its way to you tomorrow if you just act now .

What must you do? Simply send in your request for your own horoscope—remember to remind them that you are a Libra—to the Astrological Society, and they will forward it to

B
you immediately! Do it today! Don't take the chance that Pluto could be orbiting your way without your knowing it!

Astrologically yours,

John T. Libra
VRR

26. Capitalization

RULE: <u>Capitalize</u> the names of:
         A. **books**

NORR PUBLISHING COMPANY
4551 ASSOCIATION DRIVE
DALLAS, TX 11111

TELEPHONE 333 555-3124

April 11, 19--

Mrs. Louis Crandle, Chairman
Department of Administrative Services
Jon Hawkins High School
16 Downing Street
Capetown, NJ 08212

Dear Mrs. Crandle:

C   We are pleased indeed to send you for examination Gower and Mooney's *Clerical*
C, C   *Office Practice*. Since you wish to consider the text for students' use in your classes, there is
no charge.

While examining the book you may find it convenient to refer to the printed sheet
attached to the inside front cover. Teachers tell us that these sheets are a real aid in making a
careful study of NORR books.

Enclosed you will find a copy of our latest book list. We are particularly excited about
C, C, C, C   Coler's *Graded Speed Shorthand Building*. It has been very well received and is the kind of
text that schools everywhere have wanted.

To determine the net price of any NORR book, deduct the regular school discount
C, C, C   from the list price. For example, *Guide to Manners in Business* by Ellen Kiams [No.
341-417] is $11.50 after the school discount.

After you complete your examination of the materials we have sent, do let us hear
from you.

Sincerely yours,

Arthur Manley, Director
Educational Service

MW

Enclosure

27. Capitalization

> **RULE:** **Capitalize** the names of:
>
> | | |
> |---|---|
> | **D1.** hotels | **D4.** airlines |
> | **D2.** train stations | **D5.** airports |
> | **D3.** trains | **D6.** restaurants |

ITINERARY OF HILLARY FERGUSON

September 20 to 22

Memphis to Jackson

TUESDAY, SEPTEMBER 20, MEMPHIS

D5, D5, D4, D4	8:45 AM	Leave Kennedy Airport on Delta Airlines, Flight 241.
D1, D1	1:30 PM	Arrive at Memphis. Reservations for car have been made with Hertz. Hotel reservation is with Ramada Inn on Union.
	3:00 PM	Attend management conference at Cook Convention Center.
D6	7:00 PM	Meet Richard Townsend and Edwina Sanders for dinner at the Roundevous, which is within walking distance.

WEDNESDAY, SEPTEMBER 21, MEMPHIS TO JACKSON

D3	9:00 AM	Leave Memphis on Train No. 014.
	9:45 AM	Arrive at Dyersburg. Herbert Busby will meet you and drive you to his office building for a conference with the Board of Directors, CAI, Inc. Presentation of management styles will be given at this time.
	1:30 PM	Meet with representative of CAI, Inc. Union Members.
D2, D2, D2	4:55 PM	Take cab to Dyersburg Train Station.
D1	6:00 PM	Arrive at Jackson. Reservations for car at the airport. Hotel reservation at the Holidome.

THURSDAY, SEPTEMBER 22, JACKSON

	9:30 AM	Make presentation to area business executives on "Employee Motivation" in the conference room of the Holidome.
D4	2:35 PM	Depart Jackson, American, Flight 104.
	3:55 PM	Arrive Nashville. Connect with American, Flight 340.
	7:45 PM	Arrive at New York.

28. Capitalization

> **RULE:**   Capitalize the names of:
>   E. business products

KOHLMAR BUSINESS COMPUTERS
1717 NORTHSHORE DRIVE
CHICAGO, IL 60611

Telephone 333 555-4434

March 3, 19--

Sales Manager
Central Office Products, Inc.
162 North Fairbanks Court
Chicago, IL 60611

Dear Central Supply:

E, E, E, E, E

Some time ago I wrote you for franchise information regarding several business furniture product lines including Hibatchi Hard Drive Conversion Kits, Easy Control Mouses, and other items. As I have not heard from you, I wondered if my letter may have been lost.

E, E, E

I mentioned in my letter that I am expanding my computer business to include a full line of Relaxing Office Furniture and supplies. We have purchased additional mall space at considerable expense and need to finalize plans on which lines to carry.

Your products are not currently being carried by any of the local business supply outfits. I am hopeful that we can arrange a franchise to insure that our store will be the exclusive distributor of your lines of furniture in our area.

Please send me information as soon as possible, or call me at your convenience at 333 555-2001.

Sincerely,

Ernest P. Kohlmar
President

RI

29. Capitalization

> **RULE:** <u>Capitalize</u> the names of:
> F. the days of the week

AMERICAN SAFE DRIVING COUNCIL   **TELEPHONE 333 555-1001**
BOX 458
NEW YORK, NY 10021 _____

August 24, 19--

Mr. Norman Cambell
Industrial Arts Department
South High School
Lincoln, NE 68500

Dear Mr. Cambell:

Your principal, Mr. Robert Wilder, has directed us to make arrangements with you concerning an assembly program on safe driving to be held during your regular assembly
F   period any Friday during the month of September.

The usual procedure is to have our representative speak for about fifteen minutes on the importance of safe driving practices and then show a twenty-minute sound film entitled *Highway Accidents—Or Are They Accidents?* This would be followed by a demonstration of required stopping distances to be given in a nearby street. It is essential that all traffic be kept off the street during the demonstration.

F   We regret that we are unable to send a representative to your school on any Friday during
F   September or any Friday this fall. We could have our speaker-demonstrator, Mr. Arthur P.
F, F   Rentsch, present the assembly either Tuesday, October 21, or Thursday, October 30. Mr. Rentsch could spend an entire day at your school.

Please notify us if this would be satisfactory to you and which date would be most convenient. We will hold these dates for you until we hear from you again. If you can only
F   accommodate us on Friday, we can schedule you during February or anytime during the spring months.

If you have any further questions, don't hesitate to call on us.

Sincerely,

Oliver H. Seager, Director
WL

30. Capitalization

> RULE: Capitalize the names of:
>   G. the months of the year

Universal Travel
4695 Airways Blvd.
Cincinnati, OH 45200

Telephone 333 555-5678

G   August 10, 19--

Mr. Kenneth Larson
2667 Overlook Place
Cincinnati, OH 45200

Dear Mr. Larson:

G   Your Silver Jet Airlines ticket 25-620-079-200 was mailed to you on July 31. As indicated in the letter accompanying the ticket, your payment should have been received
G   within three days. As of today, August 10, our records show that your payment has not been made at this office. Please let us know if you have not received the ticket, or disregard this notice if you have already mailed your payment.

G   Perhaps your plans have changed and you find you cannot travel in September. If so, just return the ticket.

G   If we have not heard from you by August 28, we will be forced to cancel your
G   September reservation. Therefore, please take the time today to reconfirm your travel plans with us. An envelope has been enclosed for your convenience in replying.

         Thank you for letting SJA be of service to you.

Sincerely,

Osvon T. Simmons, Manager
Eastern Division

MW

Enclosure

31. Capitalization

> RULE: Capitalize the names of:
> H1. the divisions of the Bible
> H2. books of the Bible

St. Edward's Church
One Apostle Lane
Nashville, TN 37200
Telephone 333 555-2331

April 7, 19--

Dr. James Reid
22 West Broadway
Nashville, TN 37200

Dear Dr. Reid:

We are subscribers to *The Christian Monthly* and have been receiving it for many years. We feel that the material included has been inspired by God, and we congratulate you on a truly Christian magazine.

During the Easter emphasis last year, we were especially delighted with the articles concerning the Passover and with the Old Testament references to Exodus, Leviticus, and Deuteronomy. It is very important that we remember the history behind and the reasons for our celebrations.

Thank you for your hard work revealing God's love and plan for our lives. We are looking forward to reading many more issues of your magazine in the future—especially the Christmas issue.

Sincerely,

Rev. J. E. Mooney
QW

H1, H1, H2, H2
H2

32. Capitalization

> **RULE:** Capitalize the names of:
>   1. schools

August 13, 19--

Mr. Harry J. Masters, Superintendent
Greensboro Central School District
1620 Rensloe Street
Charles Town, SC 29400

Dear Mr. Masters:

We are getting ready to send our bloodmobile unit around to the different areas of our state,
and after studying last year's results, we are delighted to inform you that Greensboro Central
High School has again been chosen as the "base site" for Simmons County. The tremendous
turnout in your area last year has prompted this return.

Our unit will arrive at the high school on Monday, October 20, to set up operations for the
week. On Tuesday we will travel to Cameron Elementary School and take donations from
10:00 A.M. until 5:00 P.M. Wednesday we will follow the same schedule at Holden School.
We will vary our schedule on Thursday and Friday, locating at Poplar Bluff Junior High
School on Thursday from 9:00 A.M. until 3:00 P.M. and at Greensboro Junior High School
on Friday from 8:30 A.M. until 4:00 P.M. Donations will also be taken from 7:00 until 9:00
each evening at Greensboro Central High School.

Thank you for your cooperation. If there is a conflict on the above schedule, please let us
know, and we will make every effort to meet with you and iron out all problems. We will be
located at West Plains County School the following week.

Sincerely yours,

Maxwell Dime
Unit Coordinator

ML

33. Capitalization

RULE: **Capitalize** the names of:
J. **cities, towns, and villages**

ITINERARY FOR ALEX GAMMAS
July 16 to 18
Stillwater

MONDAY, JULY 16, TULSA

	8:00 AM	Depart Little Rock on American, Flight 125.
J	9:50 AM	Arrive at Tulsa. Meet Craig Gosher, sales representative for Apple II in the Oklahoma Restaurant of the airport.
J	2:00 PM	Depart Tulsa on Hughes Airwest, Flight 44.
J	4:15 PM	Arrive at Jonesboro. Car rental reservations are with Hertz. Lodging reservations at Ramada Inn.

TUESDAY, JULY 17, JONESBORO

9:30 AM	Attend Mid-South Convention at Arkansas State University.
11:00 AM	Make presentation at the convention on "Word Processing in Office Technology Classrooms." Afterwards, attend luncheon.
8:00 PM	Reception at ASU president's home.

WEDNESDAY, JULY 18, EVENING SHADE

	8:00 AM	Meet John Ludwick for breakfast.
	9:00 AM	Meet in your room with representatives from Business Education Publishing Co. to discuss contracts for word processing text.
J	1:05 PM	Depart Jonesboro on Frontier, Flight 22.
J, J	4:45 PM	Arrive at Evening Shade.

34. Capitalization

RULE: Capitalize the names of:
K. government offices

O R G A N I Z E D   A G E N C I E S
(Veterans' Assistance)

	Problem	Agency
	Getting former position (90 days)	Former employer or Reemployment Committee of S.S. Board
	Getting a new job: Private employer	U.S. Employment Service
K, K, K	Government	U.S. Civil Service Commission
K, K, K	Unemployment benefits	U.S.E.S. Bureau of Unemployment Compensation
	Financial aid and personal problems	American Red Cross
	Loans for homes, farms, or business	Administrator of Veterans' Affairs
K		U.S. Veterans' Administration
	Getting a pension	U.S. Veterans' Administration
	Hospital care and medical attention	U.S. Veterans' Administration
	Education and training	U.S. Veterans' Administration
		State Department of Education
	Vocational rehabilitation	U.S. Veterans' Administration
		State Department of Vocational Rehabilitation
	Legal aid and protection	Soldiers' and Sailors' Relief Commission
K, K, K		State Bar Association
K, K, K		Legal Aid Society
K, K		American Red Cross
	General information	U.S. Veterans' Information Center

35. Capitalization

RULE: **Capitalize** the names of:
    L1. historical periods
    L2. wars
    L3. holidays

Chamber of Commerce
1289 Broadway
    Hibbing, MN 55746   **Telephone 333 555-3243**

July 5, 19--

Mrs. Henry Lewis
128 Main Street
Hibbing, MN 55746

Dear Mrs. Lewis:

While in your city the Freedom Train will be open to the public from 10:00 A.M. to 10:00 P.M. daily. In its three exhibition cars, the train contains documents ranging chronologically from a letter written by Christopher Columbus, describing his discovery of the Americas, to the Charter of the United Nations, signed in 1945 and signaling the end of

L2, L2, L2, L2   World War II, and including the Gettysburg Address, written during the Civil War. Among the documents found in the nation's filing cabinet are the Mayflower Compact, the Bay Psalm Book, the original manuscript of "The Star-Spangled Banner" in the handwriting of Francis Scott Key, and Japanese and German surrender documents.

L3, L3, L3   American holidays are depicted by a special arrangement of paintings, which include not only major holidays such as the Fourth of July and Christmas but also some not-so-major

L3, L3, L3, L3   holidays such as Columbus Day and Veterans Day. There is also a special section in each car devoted to depicting such important times in America's history as the Reconstruction

L2, L2, L1, L1   following the end of the Civil War and the Great Depression of the 1930s.

I am enclosing a copy of the approved schedule and a complete list of the exhibits.

Sincerely,

Howard Brown
President

LK

Enclosure

36. Capitalization

> RULE: Capitalize the names of:
>   M. administrative bodies

THE UNITED NATIONS STRUCTURE
1988

    I. SECURITY COUNCIL: Fifteen members—the Big Five, permanent; ten elected for two-year terms by Assembly. Functions through:

        1. Atomic Energy Commission

        2. Military Staff Committee

M, M, M, M   3. International Contingents of Armed Forces

    II. GENERAL ASSEMBLY: Member nations—159. Discusses questions relating to peace, security, and other matters under Charter; makes recommendations to Security Council; functions through these specialized agencies:

M   1. Educational, Scientific, and Cultural

      2. Food and Agriculture

M   3. International Labor

M   4. International Civil Aviation

M   5. International Bank

      6. International Monetary Fund

      7. World Health

M   8. International Refugee

    III. SECRETARIAL: Secretary-General at head; includes research, administrative staffs; reports to Security Council, Assembly.

    IV. INTERNATIONAL COURT OF JUSTICE: Fifteen members chosen by the Assembly. Meets in permanent session to decide "judiciable" disputes that arise between nations.

37. Capitalization

> RULE: Capitalize the names of:
> N. courses of instruction

Patterson Free Academy
1605 Henderson Drive
Patterson, NJ 00000

Telephone 333 555-4467

March 22, 19--

Mrs. Elliott Green
246 Alto Vista Road
Waterloo, IA 50703

Dear Mrs. Green:

We shall be happy to welcome your daughter, Nancy, as one of our students when your family moves to Patterson. Since your daughter does not plan to attend college, we recommend that she enroll in our business education program. Stenographic training is an investment that can pay lifelong dividends to the person who does not want to be limited to a mediocre job. The demand for secretaries is so great that preparation in this area provides entry into every field of business and affords limitless opportunities for promotion. It is our sincere desire to perform a specific service for career-minded students.

Listed are some of the courses Nancy would be taking:

N	Keyboarding	--1133
N, N	Word Processing	--4213
N, N	Electronic Communications	--2323
	Desktop Publishing	--2533
N, N	Electronic Spreadsheets	--2632
	Principles of Economics	--2013
N, N	Principles of Accounting	--2023

If you would like a copy of a booklet describing all the courses offerings of our business education department, mail the enclosed card.

Sincerely,

William Brownholtz
Program Director

MW

Enclosure

38. Capitalization

> RULE: **Capitalize:**
>   **A.** the directions East, West, North, and South when they refer to definite sections of
>   the United States or the world or are used with other proper names
>   **B.** Avoid improper use of capitalization.

Carson Travel Bureau
South Locust Street
Carson City, CA 90746   **Telephone 333 555-2332**

June 20, 19--

Miss Ester Norman
223 Johns Avenue
San Francisco, CA 94100

Dear Miss Norman:

      Thank you very much for your enthusiastic letter of June 12. We were thrilled to learn of your interest in a trip to the Far East and would be delighted to discuss it with you.

      Our office is located on South Locust Street in nearby Carson City. We are situated in the very center of the street on the north side—you would turn left if you were facing the ocean.

      We are enclosing some descriptive literature on some of the tours we are sponsoring this fall for you to inspect (before you visit our office) to get a general idea of some plans we can make for you. We are including, as you requested, plans not only for the Far East but also for the Middle East.

      Please contact us soon so your holiday will be exactly as you wish it and you will have priority on the best accommodations—especially if you leave North America.

Sincerely yours,

Arthur Lesenberry
Manager

LDR

Enclosures

39. Capitalization

RULE: Capitalize:
   A. the directions East, West, North, and South when they refer to definite sections of the United States or are used with other proper names
   B. Avoid improper use of capitalization.

June 17, 19--

Mr. Alexander Levin
A 197 North Fifty-fifth Street
Kingston, NH 03848

Dear Mr. Levin:

Thank you for answering our ad in the *Hornell Gazette*. I hope the following information
A will help you in your decision to purchase property in West Boston.

A The town of Dennis offers "traditional" cape living. Three of the finest beaches in North
America are located here. The Bass River forms the western boundary and has several
marinas for boating enthusiasts. We are within easy access to medical facilities, since
B Boston is a short ten-minute drive east of us.

The cost of lots varies greatly, land near the water being more expensive. Waterfront lots
range from $25,000 to $30,000. However, lots located in the areas designated on the
B enclosed map sell for less, since they are south of Dennis and are in a more heavily wooded
area. These properties, though, are in beautiful year-round locations convenient to shopping, beaches, churches, and the Dennis golf course.

We have a fine selection of choice lots. Stop in and see us when you are in the area.
A Remember, the East is still a fine place to live.

Sincerely,

J. Walter White
RM
Enclosure

40. General Errors

RULE: <u>Typographical Errors:</u>
       A. typographical errors

Ground Hill Road
New Paltz, NY 12560
November 29, 19--

Ms. Kavin Graham, Caseworker
Department of Social Services
Box 1800
Kingston, NY 12404

Dear Ms. Graham:

A   This is in reference to your letter of November 2, 19--, requesting information about the
A   capabilities of Annette Corkey and Eric Adams as adoptive parents.

A, A We have known Annette as a friend, neighbor, and tenant for the past five years. We have
found her to be reliable and dependable in every way. She is a very caring individual, most
A   likely enhanced by her many years serving as a social worker.

We have known Eric for the past three years. Through his drive and determination, Eric
A   has developed a highly successful and financially sound landscape and plant maintenance
business.

Eric and Annette were married two years ago and their relationship is a close one. The
A   addition of Baby Tara to their lives only completes the picture.

Eric and Annette are both well-educated and have a great love for nature. They are fine
people who are financially, physically, and psychologically able to provide an excellent
home for Tara.

Very truly yours,

Ron and Elizabeth Kramer
RI

41. General Errors

RULE: <u>Numbers—as a general rule:</u>
  B1. spell out indefinite amounts
  B2. spell out numbers less than one hundred except dates for regular correspondence
  B3. numbers over one hundred are written in figures

A C C O U N T I N G

A Rewarding Career

Accounting is one of the largest fields of professional employment, with almost a million people working in this occupation. It is also one of the highest-paying fields of work for which a young person can prepare.

B1   A survey of more than one hundred large business organizations shows that starting
B2   salaries average over $20,000 a year. Salaries of accountants with ten years' experience are likely to be double or triple the beginning rate. Many accountants in supervisory positions
B3, B3   or self-employed accountants earn between $40,000 and $65,000 a year.

Accounting employment is expected to expand rapidly because of several factors: the general use of accounting information in an information society; business management; complex and changing tax systems; and the increasing use of accounting services by small business organizations.

Beginners in private accounting may start as ledger or cost clerks, timekeepers, junior internal auditors, or trainees for technical and executive positions. On the whole, accounting graduates are in greatest demand and are finding employment most often in small firms.

42. General Errors

RULE: **Paragraph:**
C. Each paragraph represents one complete thought.

TWENTIETH CENTURY, INC.
ONE ASSOCIATION LANE
PAOLI, OK 73074 _____

January 4, 19--

Miss Dorothy Greenleigh
2101 North Cedar Street
Paoli, OK 73074

Dear Miss Greenleigh:

The regular semiannual meeting of our General Policies Committee, of which you are a member, will be held in Delhi on Thursday and Friday, February 5 and 6.

c ¶ Kindly prepare a report covering the activities of your subcommittee since the date of our last meeting. Deliver two copies of your report to me and send one copy to each member of your subcommittee at least one week prior to the time of the meeting scheduled above.

c ¶ May I remind you that your expenses will be paid if you present vouchers with your expense account. The necessary reservation has been made for you at the Raleigh Hotel, headquarters for our meeting.

c ¶ If you have any matters that should be brought to the attention of Mr. George, please consult me about them before January 22.

Sincerely,

Clyde Anderson
General Manager

AW

43. General Errors

RULE: <u>Spelling:</u>
        D. spelling

LOADING DOCK RESPONSIBILITIES

D   1. Whenever possible, outgoing plant shipments will take priority over incoming material.

       2. When incoming supplies arrive at the plant, all efforts should be made to unload the trucks quickly in order to keep the bays open.

D, D   3. The gatekeeper, who is in charge of all truck parking, will assign a number to all incoming trucks.

D   4. If all bays are occupied when a truck arrives, the truck will be unloaded as soon as a bay is open and the truck's number is posted.

       5. Since there may be times when several trucks are waiting, offloaded material may be
D   stored on the docks in order to speed up unloading.

D   6. The dock supervisor, who is in charge of all dock operations, will determine when material may be stored in the holding areas.

D   7. As soon as dock personnel are available, the stored material will be delivered to the proper plant area.

D   8. The chief foreman who is in charge of the specific section to which the material is being delivered must sign for all material.

D   9. Delivery slips that have been properly processed must be returned to the dock supervisor by the end of each shift.

       10. If there appears to be an error on the delivery slip, notify the dock supervisor
D   immediately.

44. General Errors

> **RULE:** <u>Spelling:</u>
>   D. spelling

BIKE SAFETY RULES

D
D, D
D
D, D
D, D
D
D
D
D

Biking is almost a year-round sport or means of transportation in most areas of the nation; only ice, snow, and/or bitter cold will discourage bikers. Biking is good for fun and exercise; moreover, biking helps to save gasoline. Unfortunately, many thousands of people are seriously injured and some are killed each year in bike mishaps. A large share of the fatal accidents involve collisions with motor vehicles. Bike accidents can be prevented; in fact, a few timely reminders can help. For instance, when buying a bike be sure it is the correct size for the rider; be sure the rider can physically handle the bike. Not everyone needs a ten-speed racer. Second, be sure that the bike is mechanically sound and equipped with the proper lights, reflectors, and warning flag. Third, avoid horseplay and dangerous bike games. Fourth, be lawful—obey all traffic laws, signs, and signals; push your bike across busy intersections; always stay to the right; signal your intentions when stopping and/or turning. Fifth, don't carry large items that could block your vision or make your bike difficult to handle. Because you have the right of way doesn't mean that you have to take it if there's doubt about the actions of a nearby motor vehicle; therefore, watch for cars pulling out into traffic lanes and for people opening car doors.

45. General Errors

```
RULE:  Spelling:
       D. spelling
```

GUIDE FOR SUCCESSFUL FISHING

1. Have you taken out your tackle and checked it to make sure everything you will need

D is there and in working condition? Unless your equipment is in good order, nothing else you do will make any difference.

2. Have you made plans for where you will fish? Since some spots are better than others,

D ask around and find out where fish activity is being reported.

D 3. Is your bait fresh and luring? After all is said and done, fresh bait catches fresh fish every time!

D 4. Do you have the proper clothes for where and when you are going? Although clothes

D don't make the man or woman, being comfortable while you are fishing might make

D the trip more enjoyable.

5. Now you are ready. Don't forget to set the alarm! If you get an early start, you might

D get the early fish that are always out for their morning exercise. When the fish start

D biting, remember to keep the big ones and throw the little ones back. Above all else, be careful!

46. Review

RULES:	1. Spelling.
	2. Capitalize the first word and all nouns in the salutation.
	3. Use a comma to separate city and state in an address.
	4. Use a comma to separate the day from the year.
	5. Capitalize the first word of every sentence.
	6. Capitalize the names of administrative bodies.
	7. Use a comma after the complimentary closing when using mixed punctuation.

Lott-Shimmel Realty Company
One Realty Lane
Boulder, CO 80320

Telephone 333 555-6765

4   May 13 19--

Samuel Stevens
6 Larchment Drive
3   Boulder CO 80320
2   Dear Mr. Stevens:

Lott-Shimmel Realty Co. sells more single-family dwellings in Colorado than any other real estate agency in the state. We have twenty-one offices located in the states
1, 1   bordering Colorado in addition to the sixteen here. We sold over $350 million in residential
4   property this past year. Lott-Shimmel Realty Co. opened its first office on March 4 1948.

6   Our staff is highly trained to serve you in your effort to buy a home with a Veterans'
6, 1   Administration (VA) loan. Our computer network allows you instant access to all available homes listed in our thirty-seven offices.

Since you expressed an interest at the home show in a possible move in the near
1   future, we would be pleased to assist you in that decision. Our nearest office is located at 1200 Portland Place, in Boulder.

I would appreciate meeting with you at your earliest convenience. The summer months, traditionally the most active real estate season, are fast approaching and will afford
5   the best chance for you to sell and buy. Our office hours are listed on the enclosed card.

7   Sincerely

Ronald Kirshner
Broker

RI

Enclosure

47. Review

RULES: 1. Use a colon after each of the introductory words in the heading of a memo.
2. Use quotation marks to enclose titles of articles.
3. Use a comma to set off introductory and transition words.
4. Spelling.
5. Capitalize the first word of every sentence.
6. Each paragraph represents one complete thought.
7. Typographical error.
8. No question mark needed—not a direct question; replace with a period.

TO: Bureau Counselors

FROM: Peter Franzen, Manager

DATE: June 18, 19--

1 SUBJECT() Tips on Buying a Used Car

7   We have had so many requests in the past month for assistance and information on
2 buying and financing used cars that we have compiled a circular, ()Tips for Buying Used
2 Cars,() a copy of which is attached.

3   These circulars are now ready for use and distribution. However()before this booklet
goes in to permanent printing we would be interested in the reactions of your clients as to
7 possible additions or changes.

4   Clients who request this information should also be advised to compare costs of
5 financing any loans before they commit themselves. ()ommercial banks and credit unions
4 sometimes charge less for loans than car dealers or the finance companies through which
they do business.

6 ¶   Because charges vary according to geographic location, ask your clients to call on the
8 credit department at their own bank or credit union()

JP

48. Review

RULES: 1. Use a comma to separate the day from the year.
2. Spelling.
3. Do not spell out numbers in dates for regular correspondence.
4. Capitalize the names of months of the year.
5. Spell out numbers less than one hundred.
6. Parentheses not needed—this group of words does have direct bearing on main thought.
7. Use a comma to separate a dependent clause at the beginning of a sentence.

Natural Pools & Spas, Inc.
Box 600 State Street
Terre Haute, Indiana 47811

Telephone 333 555-9987

1   March 8 19--

CUSTOMER NAME
STREET ADDRESS
CITY, STATE ZIP CODE

Dear (CUSTOMER NAME):

This letter and the enclosed "Spring Mailer" and Chemical Coupon sheet are being sent to you as a way of thanking you for doing business with us in the past.

2, 7   With the '85 Swimming Season nearly upon us we invite you to take advantage of our
3, 2, 3   unadvertised Specials in effect from April 14 through May 13. These prices are for you, our preferred customers, and they will not be advertised in the newspaper.

2   The Natural Pools & Spas Staff is continuing to grow, yet many of the familar faces remain. Warren Angermeye, our Production Coordinator, and Joseph Silas and Georgia
2   Polishook, Salespeople, continue with us. Aditionally, our friendly office staffers Gerta Wallner and Amy Napolitano are now joined by Steven Porko.

We look forward to rewelcoming you to Natural Pools and Spas. When you visit, you
6   will notice new products have been added to our ever-expanding lines Aqua Wash,
6   Bacto-Kleen and Sea-Chem as chemicals. In addition, our Waldo Sun-Room is on display adjacent to our showroom, and four new spa lines have been added to our collection.

We will be holding several "HOMEOWNERS' POOL CHEMISTRY SEMIN-
5, 4   ARS." The first ones will be Friday, May 11 at 7:00 P.M. and then Friday, June 1 at 7:00
4   P.M. and Saturday June 2 at 10:00 A.M. and 2:00 P.M. Please plan to attend at least one seminar to refresh your "Water Chemistry." We're here to help!

Happy Swimming,

Art Newbury
President

Enclosure

RI

49. Review

RULES:
1. Use an underscore for emphasis.
2. Question mark not needed—not a direct question; replace with a period.
3. Use a hyphen to indicate a division of a word at the end of a line.
4. Capitalize the first word of every sentence.
5. Use a comma to separate a dependent clause at the beginning of a sentence.
6. Use an apostrophe for contractions.
7. Typographical error.
8. Question mark not needed—not a direct question; replace with an exclamation point.
9. Spelling.

GUIDE TO GOOD TRAVEL PICTURES

1   <u>Before You Leave</u>

9   Make sure your equipment is working properly. Check both your camera and flash to make sure the batteries are fresh. Since batteries deteriorate in certain weather conditions, be sure you have extras.

4, 2   Take enough film. Count on using at least one roll per day; two rolls, if taking movies. Carry the film with you when boarding the plane, as metal detectors used on luggage at some airports may cause exposure.

<u>Snapping That Shutter</u>

3   Watch for small details, and keep your pictures simple. Try to include a single idea. Be-
5   fore you snap your shutter, check the edges of your viewfinder for distracting objects.
6   Don't be afraid of your subject—move in close.

7   When photographing people, keep them busy. Be sure to keep your horizon level. Try to include some foreground in panoramic scenes. REMEMBER TO HOLD THE
8   CAMERA STEADY!

Have your film processed as soon as possible after it is exposed.

50. Review

RULES: 1. Use an apostrophe to indicate possessive form of nouns.
2. Typographical error.
3. Use a colon after an introductory clause that introduces an enlargement of the meaning expressed in the introductory clause.
4. Capitalize the first word of every sentence.
5. Question mark not needed—not a direct question; replace with a period.
6. Capitalize the first word in every section of an outline.
7. Spelling.
8. Numbers over one hundred are written in figures.

TIPS ON BUYING A USED CAR

1
4
2

With some routine checks and a little mechanical know-how, you should be able to get your money's worth when you buy a used car. Shop around and compare prices, cars, and dealers. A dealer who sells new cars as well as used cars is usually well-equipped to stand behind his guarantee.

A. To help you evaluate the condition of the engine:

4
7 or 2

   1. Test the engine when it is cold. If blue smoke comes from the exhaust, it could mean the engine is burning oil and needs repairs.

6 or 4
5

   2. Start from a slow speed and accelerate rapidly. If the engine jerks or balks, something may be wrong.

3

B. To help you know if the car has been in an accident:

   1. Look for signs of dents and wrinkles.

   2. Check both sides of the radiator for repair work.

7

C. To help you estimate the true mileage:

   1. Notice the condition and brand of the tires.

8

   2. Check the rubber of the brake pedal. It wears thin after 20,000 miles.

Proofreader Marks

Proofreader marks are symbols used to identify mistakes and simultaneously state the needed correction. Listed are proofreader marks, explanations of the marks, and examples.

Paragraphing

Mark	Explanation of the Mark	Example
¶	Begin a new paragraph	. . . exciting venture. ¶ Adjustments are minor.
no ¶	No new paragraph	. . . interpreted correctly no ¶ if you
fl	Flush left—Do not indent	fl < The purpose of

Spacing

Mark	Explanation of the Mark	Example
◠	Bring together	Le ave no space
#	Insert a space	Take this(or that)

Size

Mark	Explanation of the Mark	Example
lc	Use lower-case letter	The lc Small letter
≡	Use upper-case letter	proofreading material
all caps	Use upper-case letter	proofreading material all caps
/	Use lower-case letter	Proofreading Material

Proofreader Marks (continued)

Punctuation

Mark	Explanation of the Mark	Example
⊙	Place a period where indicated	I prefer artichokes⊙ He
⊙ (colon)	Place a colon where indicated	or follows⊙ (a) one
∧ (comma)	Place a comma where indicated	In addition∧ considering that he
∧ (semicolon)	Place a semicolon where indicated	. . . by graduation∧ consequently she
⊙	A circle around a punctuation mark—change to a period	I prefer brevity⊙ He will be here Monday.
=	Place a hyphen where indicated	very clear=thinking
$\frac{1}{m}$	Place a dash where indicated	animals$\frac{1}{m}$for example, the

Position

Mark	Explanation of the Mark	Example
⊐	Move to the right	⊐A copy of the proposed project is enclosed
⊏	Move to the left	⊏ Tomorrow is Tuesday, July 27. Therefore we
⊔	Lower (letters or words)	A) On occ^{a}sion a letter B) Some^{times} an entire work
⊓	Raise (letters or words)	A) Instead of flying B) The pattern was not turned
tr ∼	Transpose (letters or words)	In his rush he forgot

Insertion and Deletion

Mark	Explanation of the Mark	Example
∧	Add, insert	research studies . . . professional∧organization and
ℓ	Take out	I would before progressing
stet	Leave as originally stated	Vocational Business Education

Rules of English

Punctuation Errors

Apostrophe

Use an apostrophe:
  A. for contractions
  B. to indicate the possessive form of nouns
  C. to indicate the plural form of words referred to as words

Colon

Use a colon after:
  A. an introductory clause that introduces an enlargement of the meaning expressed in the introductory clause
  B. each of the introductory words in the heading of a memo
  C. an introductory statement containing the word *following*

Comma

Use a comma:
  A. to separate city and state in an address
  B. to separate the day from the year
  C. after the complimentary closing when using mixed punctuation
  D. to separate numbers of four or more digits
  E. to set off phrases in apposition
  F. to separate a dependent clause at the beginning of a sentence
  G. to set off introductory and transition words
  H. for clarity

Dash

Use a dash:
  A. prior to a summarizing statement
  B. to set off an independent interpolation that is a clause
  C. to set off a long appositive

Diagonal line

Use a diagonal line:
  A. to indicate the end of a line when quoting poetry
  B. when typing certain abbreviations

Exclamation Point

Use an exclamation point:
  A. after an interjection and the complete sentence when both are exclamatory
  B. to express strong emotion

Hyphen

Use a hyphen:
  A. to indicate a division of a word at the end of a line
  B. to show the omission of the word *to*
  C. to suspend the first part of a hyphenated compound
  D. in compounds containing prepositions

Parentheses

Use parentheses to:
  A. set off a group of words having no definite bearing on the main thought
  B. enclose dates indicating a period of time
  C. enclose numbers expressed in figures for clarification

Period

Use a period:
  A. at the end of a complete sentence
  B. after an abbreviation

Question Mark

Use a question mark:
  A. after a direct question

Quotation Marks

Use quotation marks to enclose:
  A. words used in a special sense
  B. technical words
  C. titles of articles

Semicolon

Use a semicolon:
  A. between series of lengthy phrases

Underscore

Use an underscore:
  A. for emphasis

Rules of English (continued)

Capitalization Errors

Capitalize the first word:

A. of every sentence
B. of every direct quotation
C. of an independent question within a sentence
D. of a phrase or sentence following a colon when:
   1. the subject matter is formal
   2. the following material is a direct quotation
E. and all nouns in the salutation
F. and all nouns in the complimentary closing
G. in every section of an outline

Capitalize the names of:

A. associations
B. astronomical bodies
C. books
D. hotels, train stations, trains, airlines, airports, and restaurants
E. business products
F. the days of the week
G. the months of the year
H. the divisions of the Bible, and books of the Bible
 I. schools
J. cities, towns, and villages
K. government offices
L. historical periods, wars, and holidays
M. administrative bodies
N. courses of instruction

Capitalize the following directions:

A. East
B. West
C. North
D. South

. . . when they refer to definite sections of the United States or the world or are used with other proper names.

General Errors:

A. Typographical errors—errors made by mistake in typing an exercise
B. Numbers—as a general rule:
   1. spell out indefinite amounts
   2. spell out numbers less than one hundred except dates for regular correspondence
   3. numbers over one hundred are written in figures
C. Paragraph—each paragraph represents one complete thought
D. Spelling—words *commonly* misspelled

Name: _____ Date: _____

Apostrophe

Directions: The business communications document below has several errors. Please proofread the document very carefully and correct all errors using the proper proofreader mark(s).

FUTURE BUSINESS LEADERS OF AMERICA
MANN HIGH SCHOOL
Agenda for Meeting, May 1, 19--
Mann High School Library, 4:00 P.M.

1. Call to Order   Jerry Abbott

2. Roll Call   Don Bramlett

3. Minutes of April Meeting   Don Bramlett

4. Report of Officers
   a. Treasurers   Gary Lunsford
   b. Vice Presidents   Albert Cressman

5. New Business   Jerry Abbott

   a. Election of new delegates
      is scheduled for our next
      meeting.

   b. The state test results from
      last year indicate that our
      chapter was weak spelling
      proper possessive plurals.
      Ex: mens—ladies. Also its
      important to avoid too
      many *ands* in the written
      communications test.

6. Adjournment   Jerry Abbott

Name: _____ Date: _____

Colon

Directions: The business communications document below has several errors. Please proofread the document very carefully and correct all errors using the proper proofreader mark(s).

TO Distributors

FROM: Consumer Products Division

DATE: March 18, 19--

SUBJECT Promotion

The following items are important points for consideration

Job progress lies in one direction: Thorough training and the ability to adapt to ever-changing needs will invariably encourage advancement.

You are in a powerful role: You represent a multimillion-dollar company that is the leader in the field of home-care products.

We offer eighty-three products under eight general care areas Personal, Furniture, Floor, Rug and Carpet, General Home, Odor Control, Insect Control, and Car.

Note that we plan to open three new areas in the next year: Laundry Care, Wall and Ceiling Care, and Basement Playroom Care.

Distributors must have a complete knowledge of all products Classes to demonstrate and learn about new products will meet monthly.

The following will increase your regular sales; Complete knowledge of all products, completion of the sales promotion seminar program, and, of course, hard work and dedication.

The goal of becoming a gold-level distributor lies ahead; Mastering the product line, determination, and our strong leadership can assure your place among the select.

BP

Name: _____ Date: _____

Comma

Directions: The business communications document below has several errors. Please proofread the document very carefully and correct all errors using the proper proofreader marks(s).

ELCO FUEL OIL COMPANY	**Telephone**	**DAYS**	**212 555-2314**
1002 Energy Lane		**NIGHTS**	**212 555-2333**
Satsop, WA		**EMERGENCY**	**212 555-2222**

COAL • COMMERCIAL OIL • HOME HEATING OIL • KEROSENE

August 9 19--

Mr. Charles K. Bruce
Ideal Toy Company
49 Harding Avenue
Satsop WA 98583

Dear Mr. Bruce:

You are correct in estimating that you use over 9000 gallons of No. 2 fuel oil each year to heat your building. The cost is high; we agree.

Perhaps you should consider converting to No. 5 fuel oil and a Duncan Heavy-Oil Burner. By so doing; you could save up to 7 cents on each gallon. Actually; though the heavier oil costs less per gallon than the lighter oil it gives 15% more heat. Furthermore; the Duncan Burner is efficient and dependable. Last year over 10000 burners were converted to take advantage of the savings.

The enclosed circular shows the yearly savings on some typical installations that we have recently converted. If you are interested we shall be glad to show you any of these installations and to arrange a meeting with the satisfied purchaser.

Sincerely

Edward J. Warren
Sales Manager

FD

Enclosure

Name: _____ Date: _____

Dash

Directions: The business communications document below has several errors. Please proofread the document very carefully and correct all errors using the proper proofreader mark(s).

PARKHILL SAVINGS BANK
1372 Rollins Drive
Springfield, VT 05156
Telephone 555 333-9009

June 15, 19--

Mr. Thomas Raynor
264 Brandon Street
Springfield, VT 05156

Dear Mr. Raynor:

Permit me to extend a friendly greeting to you as a member of our large family of depositors. We appreciate your patronage and trust that you will make use of the various services that the Parkhill Savings Bank offers.

I wish particularly to bring to your attention one of our newer facilities "over-the-counter" SAVINGS BANK LIFE INSURANCE. Few people are aware that life insurance can be coupled with a long-range savings account. This type of insurance believe it or not provides unusual policy benefits, yet the net cost is low because no selling commissions are paid.

On your next visit to our bank, why not make inquiry at the Life Insurance desk about the type of insurance best suited to your needs? We don't want you—or any of our customers—to lose your home, your land holdings, your personal investments all your lifetime acquirements because of negligence on our part. I am sure you will be pleasantly surprised to learn of the many advantages of SAVINGS BANK INSURANCE.

Please accept my cordial good wishes. We shall look forward to serving you for a long time to come.

Sincerely yours,

Howard Dunnigan
President

WO

Name: _____ Date: _____

Diagonal Line

Directions: The business communications document below has several errors. Please proofread the document very carefully and correct all errors using the proper proofreader mark(s).

————————————— **MEMO** —————————————

TO: All Employees

FROM: Fred Simpson, President

DATE: January 26, 19--

SUBJECT: Correspondence

In dating future correspondence, please remember the following; "Thirty days hath September, April, June, and November, February hath twenty-eight alone, And all the rest have thirty-one."

All mail for Howard Brown should be sent to John Johnson, c o Station WCBQ, Independence, IA.

JT

Name: _____ Date: _____

Exclamation Point

Directions: The business communications document below has several errors. Please proofread the document very carefully and correct all errors using the proper proofreader marks(s).

BIG 10 STORES
Bald Knob, Jonesboro, Newburgh, Walden, and Warwick

CUSTOMER'S NAME
STREET ADDRESS
CITY, STATE ZIP CODE

Dear LAST NAME:

To help FIRNAME get the most out of HIS/HER money we are having a special "Products Give-A-Way" on Thursday evening, October 16th. Oh, what bargains are in store for you Every item in the store will be specially marked, and certain items will be red-tagged for Super Savings Enclosed you will find five coupons that you may use to receive additional savings on any item you choose. Save those coupons You won't want to miss a single opportunity to increase your shopping value and further your savings.

In order to prepare ourselves for this spectacular event, we will be closed from 1:00 to 6:00 P.M. on October 15. If you have any questions about the event, don't hesitate to call. Our switchboard operators will be prepared to answer any and all inquiries.

We are looking forward to the pleasure of your presence at our "Products Give-A-Way." Don't forget October 16, and don't forget your coupons

See you there

MANAGER'S NAME
Store Manager

SERVING OUR CUSTOMERS BETTER

Name: _____ Date: _____

Hyphen

Directions: The business communications document below has several errors. Please proofread the document very carefully and correct all errors using the proper proofreader marks(s).

TO: All Personnel

FROM: President Howell

DATE: May 8, 19--

SUBJECT: Board of Directors Meeting--May 25, 19--

Plans are being made for the Board of Directors meeting to be held the end of this month (May 25, 10 2). Ex-president Whitlow will be in attendance to help facilitate preparation for the change in-policy statements. All chairpersons of the departments involved need to get their reports into my office on Monday.

We will be discussing short and long-term contracts; some additional benefits for two, three, and four member housholds; the possibility of a once- or twice-monthly bulletin to de partments with vital news and information; complaints that have been turned in to the vice president's office; and the formation of a three or five-member buffer team to improve relations between the working staff and the president's office.

Please have your input for the above items of discussion ready and turned in to the vice president's office by the 1st also.

Thank you.

DFW

Name: _____   Date: _____

Parentheses

Directions: The business communications document below has several errors. Please proofread the document very carefully and correct all errors using the proper proofreader marks(s).

BUYING A HOME

How to Assess Your Housing Needs

More than 64% of all American families own their homes, and the percentage is growing. See figs. 1 and 2. Perhaps your family is planning to become involved in what will possibly be its largest purchase ever.

Owning a home gives many people a sense of security. During the Browning era 1785-1880 it was established that homeowners take great pride in ownership and find satisfaction in maintaining their property. Buying a home is often regarded as one of the soundest investments a family can make.

Disadvantages should also be carefully considered before taking the big step. It is more difficult to move when you own than when you rent. Home ownership entails financial risk as well as extra work and expense. In addition to the substantial drain on savings resulting from the purchase, maintenance costs must be taken into account.

Which is best for your family—to buy or rent? Weigh the pro and cons so that your decision does not verge on impulse. For further information and advice, send us twenty-five 25 dollars with your name and address and we will be delighted to set up a consultation for you with our lawyers.

Better Homes Bureau

Name: _____   Date: _____

Period

Directions: The business communications document below has several errors. Please proofread the document very carefully and correct all errors using the proper proofreader marks(s).

ITINERARY OF BILL HUTCHINSON

March 18 to 21

Atlanta to Miami

MONDAY, MARCH 18, ATLANTA

9:15 AM   Depart Birmingham on Pan Am, Flight 142.

10:00 AM   Arrive at Atlanta. Meet with Frank Deloach to discuss contract terms for Clark Co at the Airport Restaurant. Frank will drive you to Stouffer's Inn, where your room is reserved

3:00 PM   Meet with Garry George to discuss possibilities of production expansion at the Vans Co, Atlanta branch.

TUESDAY, MARCH 19, ATLANTA TO GAINESVILLE

8:35 AM   Depart Atlanta on TWA, Flight 35

10:30 AM   Arrive at Gainesville Reservations for rental car have been made with Avis. Drive to Evans Inc, Gainesville branch, to meet with plant manager, Kenneth Bentley.

WEDNESDAY, MARCH 20, GAINESVILLE TO MIAMI

9:00 AM   Depart Gainesville on Delta, Flight 751.

10:35 AM   Arrive at Miami. Reservations for room have been made with Hilton Fountainebleu Rent car at the airport.

1:00 PM   Meet with Ray Hall to discuss possibilities of opening Pool and Spa Ltd branch in Miami.

THURSDAY, MARCH 21, MIAMI TO BIRMINGHAM

8:35 AM   Depart Miami on Delta, Flight 101

11:00 AM   Connect in Atlanta, Delta, Flight 49.

1:20 PM   Arrive in Birmingham.

    13   *Proofreading Practice*

Name: _____   Date: _____

Question Mark

Directions: The business communications document below has several errors. Please proofread the document very carefully and correct all errors using the proper proofreader marks(s).

DEATSMAN & MARTIN, INC.   **Telephone 333 555-8712**
9685 Melody Lane
Venus, PA 16364 _____

December 20, 19--

Mrs. Frank S. Johnson
19 Wayne Street
Venus, PA 16364

Dear Mrs. Johnson:

Have you often wondered if your child would enjoy learning to play the piano. Have you hesitated to do anything about it, however, because you thought it would be too expensive! If so, you will surely be interested in learning about our unusual offer.

We will lend you a new piano for two weeks with no obligation on your part. The piano will be delivered to your home, and we will provide a qualified teacher who will give your child two piano lessons absolutely free.

If you would prefer a longer trial period, you may select a piano on a rental basis, and we will provide 12 free lessons for your child. The entire amount paid as a rental fee will be applied to the selling price should you decide to purchase the piano at the end of the trial period.

We invite you to visit our Music Department to discuss the many advantages of this offer. You will then have an opportunity to see and hear a selection of pianos from the world's most renowned piano manufacturers. Sound interesting. Call immediately for an appointment.

Sincerely,

Jerome Q. Hayes, Manager
Music Department

VSD

14   *Proofreading Practice*

Name: _____ Date: _____

Quotation Marks

Directions: The business communications document below has several errors. Please proofread the document very carefully and correct all errors using the proper proofreader marks(s).

ACID RAIN—A TIME BOMB

The term acid rain, coined by Angus Smith, a 19th-century Scottish scientist, has become the environmental problem of the 80s.

George Handley of Bookhaven Institute, who has conducted studies around the world, reports that atmospheric sulfur concentrations are a problem in the entire Northern Hemisphere and parts of the Southern Hemisphere.

The problem seems especially bad in America's Northeast. Industries and utilities in the Midwest spew sulfur dioxide and oxides of nitrogen into the troposphere, where they enter the jet stream and travel eastward. These sulfate and nitrate particles combine with water during any form of precipitation to form sulfuric and nitric acids.

Ohio produces 9,000 tons of sulfur dioxide daily. This amounts to twice the total output of the six New England states, New York, and New Jersey combined.

The Adirondacks, where already over 250 lakes are dead (devoid of fish life due to acidity), have acid levels that measured 3.54 pH, which is equivalent to the juice of a dill pickle.

The area from the Catskill Mountains to the Atlantic Ocean has been experiencing increased acidity levels despite local control of pollutants. In addition to water contamination of lake and streams, other problems have surfaced.

Some of our most beloved landmarks, such as the Statue of Liberty, are being eroded by the rains. Stone buildings like the Metropolitan Museum may need a total facelift every five years if the acid level in the precipitation remains as high as it is now.

Other studies in southern New York State show that the rain is wearing away the natural waxy coating on leaves of most plants, leaving them more susceptible to fungus diseases. Once again modern humanity has created a monster, and humanity must now come up with solutions to combat this problem.

For additional information, read the article Producing Acid Rain by Thomas Dew in the latest issue of the *Journal of Forestry*.

Name: _____ Date: _____

Semicolon

Directions: The business communications document below has several errors. Please proofread the document very carefully and correct all errors using the proper proofreader marks(s).

FALLS ELECTRICAL COMPANY
45 BROADWAY   **Telephone 333 555-0092**
LOS ALAMOS, NM 87544

June 7, 19--

The Buffalo Record
82 Niagara Street
Los Alamos, NM 87544

Attention: Advertising Department

Gentlemen:

Kindly place the following advertisements in the Classified Advertisements Supplement of your paper on Sunday, June 23. The articles are to be placed in the HELP WANTED section.

> STENOGRAPHER-TYPIST, able to take rapid dictation and do general office work starting salary, $235 permanent position and good chance for advancement; experience not essential, but must be willing and easily adaptable reply with complete qualifications. Box . . ., RECORD

> INDIVIDUAL, high school graduate, knowledge of typing, shorthand, and Spanish export dept. experience unnecessary; $1,355 a month reply with complete details. Box . . ., RECORD

Please assign individual "Box Numbers" to each of these inserts and send this information to us. You will, of course, charge these insertions to our account.

Sincerely,

Eugene Fischer
Personnel Director

EN

Name: _____ Date: _____

Underscore

Directions: The business communications document below has several errors. Please proofread the document very carefully and correct all errors using the proper proofreader marks(s).

PARKHILL SAVINGS BANK

A Guide to Our Services

1. Insured Savings. Individual accounts insured by Federal Deposit Insurance Corporation up to $100,000; joint accounts up to $200,000.

2. Banking by Mail. The easy way to save regularly. Safe, convenient, timesaving.

3. Mortgage Loans. F.H.A. insured. Long terms, easy payments.

4. Savings Bank Money Orders. Cost, only $2.00 each for any amount up to $1,000.

5. Safe-Deposit Boxes. Yearly rental, $9.50 and up (plus tax).

6. Traveler's Checks. Protection for your funds while you travel.

7. Christmas Club. For Christmas and other year-end expenses. Deposit of $.50 weekly and up accepted.

8. Savings Bank Life Insurance. Full protection at low cost. Liberal dividends. All types of policies available.

9. Foreign Remittances. Reasonable rates on money orders, checks, radio, cable.

Name: _____ Date: _____

Sentence

Directions: The business communications document below has several errors. Please proofread the document very carefully and correct all errors using the proper proofreader mark(s).

PLAY REVIEW

Last night I saw an exciting new play entitled *It's in the Wind*. never before have I seen such an engaging performance by a newcomer to the stage as I did last night. It was brief; but, oh yes, I'll never forget it. susan Greer (don't forget that name) is a natural. My theatre partner said, "She makes me want to just hold her in my arms and protect her from all the injustices that are sure to come her way." i agreed and then I heard someone sitting behind me say, "Don't you feel sorry for the rest of the cast? they can't compare their performance with Susan's." So I feel compelled to say something about the rest of the cast. They were marvelous. If they hadn't been, then Susan's presentation of the lead would have surely fallen short without the support from the rest of the players. for one to come away from a play so thoroughly enjoyable and hear fellow members of the audience say, "I'm coming back as soon as I can get a seat," you have to realize the entire cast was superb.

What else can I say? Oh, what a performance! don't miss it!

Name: _____ Date: _____

Direct Quotation

Directions: The business communications document below has several errors. Please proofread the document very carefully and correct all errors using the proper proofreader mark(s).

DORIGHT CORPORATION, LTD.
212 High Street
Westfield, MA 01085
333 555-4441

April 24, 19--

Mr. Vito White
27 Paddock Place
Westfield, MA 01085

Dear Mr. White:

When did you last tell your staff, "things have to improve around here or some heads will roll"? Are you always forced to be on top of things at the office when you would rather be out in the community furthering your "community relations"?

If you answered "never" or "no" to the questions above, then you may not need our services, but if you answered "occasionally" or "yes," then we feel sure you need us. We have made a survey that we think you will be interested in. It includes the problems mentioned in addition to many other business entanglements.

You are now asking, "what must I do to take advantage of this offer?" Simply send us a short letter stating your needs, and we will forward you all the information we have that even remotely concerns your problem area.

Thank you for your interest.

Sincerely,

Jonathan Doright
President

LD

Name: _____ Date: _____

Independent Questions Within a Sentence

Directions: The business communications document below has several errors. Please proofread the document very carefully and correct all errors using the proper proofreader mark(s).

STUDENTS, NOW HEAR THIS!

Are you often faced with the question, when am I going to get this term paper finished? Or have you ever asked yourself, how will I ever get the answers to these questions with the class load I have?

Many of you have a pretty full day—would you believe one study hall a week? Often you find you've used your last study hall and that library assignment is due tomorrow. The library doesn't close at the end of the eighth period; you can stay until 4:30 and take the academic bus home.

Some materials you will need for research may not be taken from the library during the school day, but they may be signed out at the close of school for overnight. Both general and special encyclopedias as well as the reserve book collection are in this category. So don't stand around complaining. Come on in and get busy. There is no reason you should ask, where is the opportunity I need to get ahead? We're always here.

In addition to fiction, nonfiction, and the familiar biographies, you will find reference books such as atlases, almanacs, dictionaries, thesauri, and secretarial handbooks. We also have books of quotations and books on music, art, and etiquette.

Your library has more than just books. Don't forget periodicals, which may be signed out for a period of two weeks. You may wish to consult the vertical file when doing research work on facts not in book form such as maps, paintings, and art reproductions. Use the record collection, the transparencies, and the filmstrips.

If you aren't sure about a book, just ask us questions such as, what is a thesaurus and how can it help me? We are here just to answer such questions and to help you use all the library facilities to their fullest.

Never hesitate to ask us for help!

The Librarians

READ FOR KNOWLEDGE

Name: _____ Date: _____

Phrase or Sentence Following a Colon

Directions: The business communications document below has several errors. Please proofread the document very carefully and correct all errors using the proper proofreader mark(s).

AMERICAN SAFE DRIVING COUNCIL   **TELEPHONE 333 555-1001**
BOX 458
NEW YORK, NY 10021

August 19, 19--

Mr. James H. Wetherell, Principal
Susquehanna High School
Susquehanna, PA 18847

Dear Mr. Wetherell:

You undoubtedly share the concern of responsible citizens over the fact that carelessness on the highways annually results in many deaths. Last year 41,000 people in the United States lost their lives as the direct result of automobile accidents. As our Highway Commissioner has often said: "we must have a continuing campaign for safe driving on our nation's highways."

Although drivers under age twenty-five represent 15% of all drivers, they account for 25% of the accidents. We would like to enlist your support in the promotion of safe driving among your high school students.

Our program consists of promoting an awareness of: automobile accident statistics, the importance of having a safe vehicle, and the importance of being a safe driver.

We can provide each student in your school with a copy of the enclosed brochure. If you would like to have one of our safe driving instructors put on a demonstration at your school, please write us.

We hope your school will soon share our motto: be smart, be sure, be safe.

Sincerely,

Oliver H. Seager
Director

EP

Enclosure

Note: An early response will assure you of a greater opportunity of scheduling on the date of
       your choice.

Name: _____ Date: _____

Salutation and Complimentary Closing

Directions: The business communications document below has several errors. Please proofread the document very carefully and correct all errors using the proper proofreader mark(s).

September 14, 19--

Mr. Harry Gelatt
President
Rotary Club of Chugwater
143 Main Street
Chugwater, WY 82210

dear mr. gellatt:

We have embarked on a campaign to reduce the number of deaths occurring each year as a result of automobile accidents. We are seeking the support of local service organizations in publicizing the factors that contribute to the tragic traffic picture.

Our Speakers' Bureau is devoting its entire attention this year to traffic safety. Each speaker is prepared to present an illustrated lecture stressing the principal causes of traffic fatalities. Among the points discussed are: city traffic, driving on expressways, stopping distances, and holiday driving. The talk will emphasize the precautions drivers should observe to protect their own lives and the lives of others.

After you read the enclosed publicity release, we feel sure you will want to hear one of our speakers.

sincerely yours,

Oliver H. Seager
Director

KR

Enclosure

DRIVE SMART ------------------------ DON'T BE A DUMMY

Name: _____ Date: _____

Outline Sections

Directions: The business communications document below has several errors. Please proofread the document very carefully and correct all errors using the proper proofreader mark(s).

GUIDES FOR SAFE DRIVING

Do you want to be a good driver? If you do, you will want to practice the following safe driving techniques:

Don't:

1. Drive with a dirty windshield or one cluttered with stickers.

2. Drive when you are sleepy, angry, or depressed.

3. pass on curves or hills.

4. allow too many people to get in your car.

5. "tailgate."

6. Be a "show-off" while driving a car.

7. Cut in too soon after passing another car.

8. Drive after having an alcoholic drink.

Do:

1. Drive at lower speeds on slippery highways, in heavy traffic, and in bad weather.

2. Have good lights and dim them when traffic approaches.

3. pay attention to stop signs, highway signs, or danger signs.

4. Have your brakes checked regularly.

5. Signal before you start, pass, stop, or back up.

6. keep your mind on your driving, your eyes on the road, and your hands on the steering wheel.

7. have good tires on all wheels.

8. Be a courteous driver!

Name: _____ Date: _____

Associations

Directions: The business communications document below has several errors. Please proofread the document very carefully and correct all errors using the proper proofreader mark(s).

The community council
Box 54621
Davenport, ND 58021

333 555-9009

February 10, 19--

Mr. & Mrs. Walter Morgan
67 Oak Street
Davenport, ND 58021

Dear Citizens:

Your community council has invited the american red cross to send a speaker to our July Open Meeting.

The local chapter has graciously offered to send us a field representative who will talk about some of the work in which the red cross is most interested at the present time. Although we have general information about the excellent work this organization is doing, it should be most interesting and valuable to hear first-hand details from a worker just returned from an actual combat zone.

The meeting will be held at the Hotel Sampson at Main and Tenth streets.

Will you make a special effort to be there promptly at 8:00 P.M. on Thursday, July 6?

Sincerely,

Henry S. Blake
Chairman

DH

Name: _____ Date: _____

Astronomical Bodies

Directions: The business communications document below has several errors. Please proofread the document very carefully and correct all errors using the proper proofreader mark(s).

February 22, 19--

Amos R. Libra
2516 Legal Circle
Carson City, CA 89701

Dear Fellow Libra:

Have you ever taken advantage of the services offered by the Astrological Society to which you belong? Have you let them give you a complete ''astrological check-up'' to determine if your future includes an alignment with mars or if you will get caught up in the milky way and have a hard time relating to others in the galaxy?

We are now offering to you a special once-a-year deal where we can keep you informed of the year's events and the chances of Libra running into trouble with Serpens, the Snake. Your horoscope could be on its way to you tomorrow if you just act now .

What must you do? Simply send in your request for your own horoscope—remember to remind them that you are a Libra—to the Astrological Society, and they will forward it to you immediately! Do it today! Don't take the chance that pluto could be orbiting your way without your knowing it!

Astrologically yours,

John T. Libra

VRR

Name: _____ Date: _____

Books

Directions: The business communications document below has several errors. Please proofread the document very carefully and correct all errors using the proper proofreader mark(s).

NORR PUBLISHING COMPANY
4551 ASSOCIATION DRIVE
DALLAS, TX 11111

TELEPHONE 333 555-3124

April 11, 19--

Mrs. Louis Crandle, Chairman
Department of Administrative Services
Jon Hawkins High School
16 Downing Street
Capetown, NJ 08212

Dear Mrs. Crandle:

We are pleased indeed to send you for examination Gower and Mooney's *clerical office practice*. Since you wish to consider the text for students' use in your classes, there is no charge.

While examining the book you may find it convenient to refer to the printed sheet attached to the inside front cover. Teachers tell us that these sheets are a real aid in making a careful study of NORR books.

Enclosed you will find a copy of our latest book list. We are particularly excited about Coler's *graded speed shorthand building*. It has been very well received and is the kind of text that schools everywhere have wanted.

To determine the net price of any NORR book, deduct the regular school discount from the list price. For example, *guide to manners in business* by Ellen Kiams [No. 341-417] is $11.50 after the school discount.

After you complete your examination of the materials we have sent, do let us hear from you.

Sincerely yours,

Arthur Manley, Director
Educational Service

MW

Enclosure

26

Name: _____ Date: _____

Hotels, Train Stations, Trains, Airlines, Airports, and Restaurants

Directions: The business communications document below has several errors. Please proofread the document very carefully and correct all errors using the proper proofreader mark(s).

ITINERARY OF HILLARY FERGUSON

September 20 to 22

Memphis to Jackson

TUESDAY, SEPTEMBER 20, MEMPHIS

8:45 AM   Leave kennedy airport on delta airlines, Flight 241.

1:30 PM   Arrive at Memphis. Reservations for car have been made with Hertz. Hotel reservation is with ramada inn on Union.

3:00 PM   Attend management conference at Cook Convention Center.

7:00 PM   Meet Richard Townsend and Edwina Sanders for dinner at the roundevous, which is within walking distance.

WEDNESDAY, SEPTEMBER 21, MEMPHIS TO JACKSON

9:00 AM   Leave Memphis on train No. 014.

9:45 AM   Arrive at Dyersburg. Herbert Busby will meet you and drive you to his office building for a conference with the Board of Directors, CAI, Inc. Presentation of management styles will be given at this time.

1:30 PM   Meet with representative of CAI, Inc. Union Members.

4:55 PM   Take cab to dyersburg train station.

6:00 PM   Arrive at Jackson. Reservations for car at the airport. Hotel reservation at the holidome.

THURSDAY, SEPTEMBER 22, JACKSON

9:30 AM   Make presentation to area business executives on "Employee Motivation" in the conference room of the Holidome.

2:35 PM   Depart Jackson, american, Flight 104.

3:55 PM   Arrive Nashville. Connect with American, Flight 340.

7:45 PM   Arrive at New York.

Name: _____ Date: _____

Business Products

Directions: The business communications document below has several errors. Please proofread the document very carefully and correct all errors using the proper proofreader mark(s).

KOHLMAR BUSINESS COMPUTERS
1717 NORTHSHORE DRIVE
CHICAGO, IL 60611

Telephone 333 555-4434

March 3, 19--

Sales Manager
Central Office Products, Inc.
162 North Fairbanks Court
Chicago, IL 60611

Dear Central Supply:

Some time ago I wrote you for franchise information regarding several business furniture product lines including hibatchi hard Drive Conversion Kits, easy control mouses, and other items. As I have not heard from you, I wondered if my letter may have been lost.

I mentioned in my letter that I am expanding my computer business to include a full line of relaxing office furniture and supplies. We have purchased additional mall space at considerable expense and need to finalize plans on which lines to carry.

Your products are not currently being carried by any of the local business supply outfits. I am hopeful that we can arrange a franchise to insure that our store will be the exclusive distributor of your lines of furniture in our area.

Please send me information as soon as possible, or call me at your convenience at 333 555-2001.

Sincerely,

Ernest P. Kohlmar
President

RI

Name: _____   Date: _____

Days of the Week

Directions: The business communications document below has several errors. Please proofread the document very carefully and correct all errors using the proper proofreader mark(s).

AMERICAN SAFE DRIVING COUNCIL   **TELEPHONE 333 555-1001**
BOX 458
NEW YORK, NY 10021 _____

August 24, 19--

Mr. Norman Cambell
Industrial Arts Department
South High School
Lincoln, NE 68500

Dear Mr. Cambell:

Your principal, Mr. Robert Wilder, has directed us to make arrangements with you concerning an assembly program on safe driving to be held during your regular assembly period any friday during the month of September.

The usual procedure is to have our representative speak for about fifteen minutes on the importance of safe driving practices and then show a twenty-minute sound film entitled *Highway Accidents—Or Are They Accidents?* This would be followed by a demonstration of required stopping distances to be given in a nearby street. It is essential that all traffic be kept off the street during the demonstration.

We regret that we are unable to send a representative to your school on any friday during September or any friday this fall. We could have our speaker-demonstrator, Mr. Arthur P. Rentsch, present the assembly either tuesday, October 21, or thursday, October 30. Mr. Rentsch could spend an entire day at your school.

Please notify us if this would be satisfactory to you and which date would be most convenient. We will hold these dates for you until we hear from you again. If you can only accommodate us on friday, we can schedule you during February or anytime during the spring months.

If you have any further questions, don't hesitate to call on us.

Sincerely,

Oliver H. Seager, Director

WL

Name: _____ Date: _____

Months of the Year

Directions: The business communications document below has several errors. Please proofread the document very carefully and correct all errors using the proper proofreader mark(s).

Universal Travel
4695 Airways Blvd.
Cincinnati, OH 45200

Telephone 333 555-5678

---

august 10, 19--

Mr. Kenneth Larson
2667 Overlook Place
Cincinnati, OH 45200

Dear Mr. Larson:

Your Silver Jet Airlines ticket 25-620-079-200 was mailed to you on july 31. As indicated in the letter accompanying the ticket, your payment should have been received within three days. As of today, august 10, our records show that your payment has not been made at this office. Please let us know if you have not received the ticket, or disregard this notice if you have already mailed your payment.

Perhaps your plans have changed and you find you cannot travel in september. If so, just return the ticket.

If we have not heard from you by august 28, we will be forced to cancel your september reservation. Therefore, please take the time today to reconfirm your travel plans with us. An envelope has been enclosed for your convenience in replying.

Thank you for letting SJA be of service to you.

Sincerely,

Osvon T. Simmons, Manager
Eastern Division

MW

Enclosure

Name: _____ Date: _____

Divisions of the Bible, Books of the Bible

Directions: The business communications document below has several errors. Please proofread the document very carefully and correct all errors using the proper proofreader mark(s).

St. Edward's Church
One Apostle Lane
Nashville, TN 37200
Telephone 333 555-2331

April 7, 19--

Dr. James Reid
22 West Broadway
Nashville, TN 37200

Dear Dr. Reid:

We are subscribers to *The Christian Monthly* and have been receiving it for many years. We feel that the material included has been inspired by God, and we congratulate you on a truly Christian magazine.

During the Easter emphasis last year, we were especially delighted with the articles concerning the Passover and with the old testament references to exodus, leviticus, and deuteronomy. It is very important that we remember the history behind and the reasons for our celebrations.

Thank you for your hard work revealing God's love and plan for our lives. We are looking forward to reading many more issues of your magazine in the future—especially the Christmas issue.

Sincerely,

Rev. J. E. Mooney

QW

Name: _____   Date: _____

Schools

Directions: The business communications document below has several errors. Please proofread the document very carefully and correct all errors using the proper proofreader mark(s).

August 13, 19--

Mr. Harry J. Masters, Superintendent
Greensboro Central School District
1620 Rensloe Street
Charles Town, SC 29400

Dear Mr. Masters:

We are getting ready to send our bloodmobile unit around to the different areas of our state, and after studying last year's results, we are delighted to inform you that greensboro central high school has again been chosen as the "base site" for Simmons County. The tremendous turnout in your area last year has prompted this return.

Our unit will arrive at the high school on Monday, October 20, to set up operations for the week. On Tuesday we will travel to cameron elementary school and take donations from 10:00 A.M. until 5:00 P.M. Wednesday we will follow the same schedule at holden school. We will vary our schedule on Thursday and Friday, locating at poplar bluff junior high school on Thursday from 9:00 A.M. until 3:00 P.M. and at greensboro Junior High School on Friday from 8:30 A.M. until 4:00 P.M. Donations will also be taken from 7:00 until 9:00 each evening at greensboro central high School.

Thank you for your cooperation. If there is a conflict on the above schedule, please let us know, and we will make every effort to meet with you and iron out all problems. We will be located at West Plains County School the following week.

Sincerely yours,

Maxwell Dime
Unit Coordinator

ML

Name: _____ Date: _____

Cities, Towns, and Villages

Directions: The business communications document below has several errors. Please proofread the document very carefully and correct all errors using the proper proofreader mark(s).

ITINERARY FOR ALEX GAMMAS

July 16 to 18

Stillwater

MONDAY, JULY 16, TULSA

8:00 AM   Depart Little Rock on American, Flight 125.

9:50 AM   Arrive at tulsa. Meet Craig Gosher, sales representative for Apple II in the Oklahoma Restaurant of the airport.

2:00 PM   Depart tulsa on Hughes Airwest, Flight 44.

4:15 PM   Arrive at jonesboro. Car rental reservations are with Hertz. Lodging reservations at Ramada Inn.

TUESDAY, JULY 17, JONESBORO

9:30 AM   Attend Mid-South Convention at Arkansas State University.

11:00 AM   Make presentation at the convention on "Word Processing in Office Technology Classrooms." Afterwards, attend luncheon.

8:00 PM   Reception at ASU president's home.

WEDNESDAY, JULY 18, EVENING SHADE

8:00 AM   Meet John Ludwick for breakfast.

9:00 AM   Meet in your room with representatives from Business Education Publishing Co. to discuss contracts for word processing text.

1:05 PM   Depart jonesboro on Frontier, Flight 22.

4:45 PM   Arrive at evening shade.

Name: _____ Date: _____

Government Offices

Directions: The business communications document below has several errors. Please proofread the document very carefully and correct all errors using the proper proofreader mark(s).

O R G A N I Z E D   A G E N C I E S
(Veterans' Assistance)

<u>Problem</u>	<u>Agency</u>
Getting former position (90 days)	Former employer or Reemployment Committee of S.S. Board
Getting a new job: Private employer Government	U.S. Employment Service U.S. civil service commission
Unemployment benefits	U.S.E.S. bureau of unemployment compensation
Financial aid and personal problems	American Red Cross
Loans for homes, farms, or business	Administrator of Veterans' Affairs U.S. veterans' Administration
Getting a pension	U.S. Veterans' Administration
Hospital care and medical attention	U.S. Veterans' Administration
Education and training	U.S. Veterans' Administration State Department of Education
Vocational rehabilitation	U.S. Veterans' Administration State Department of Vocational Rehabilitation
Legal aid and protection	Soldiers' and Sailors' Relief Commission state bar association legal aid society American red cross
General information	U.S. Veterans' Information Center

Name: _____ Date: _____

Historical Periods, Wars, and Holidays

Directions: The business communications document below has several errors. Please proofread the document very carefully and correct all errors using the proper proofreader mark(s).

Chamber of Commerce
   1289 Broadway
      Hibbing, MN 55746   **Telephone 333 555-3243**

July 5, 19--

Mrs. Henry Lewis
128 Main Street
Hibbing, MN 55746

Dear Mrs. Lewis:

While in your city the Freedom Train will be open to the public from 10:00 A.M. to 10:00 P.M. daily. In its three exhibition cars, the train contains documents ranging chronologically from a letter written by Christopher Columbus, describing his discovery of the Americas, to the Charter of the United Nations, signed in 1945 and signaling the end of world war II, and including the Gettysburg Address, written during the civil war. Among the documents found in the nation's filing cabinet are the Mayflower Compact, the Bay Psalm Book, the original manuscrupt of "The Star-Spangled Banner" in the handwriting of Francis Scott Key, and Japanese and German surrender documents.

American holidays are depicted by a special arrangement of paintings, which include not only major holidays such as the fourth of july and christmas but also some not-so-major holidays such as columbus day and veterans day. There is also a special section in each car devoted to depicting such important times in America's history as the Reconstruction following the end of the civil war and the great depression of the 1930s.

I am enclosing a copy of the approved schedule and a complete list of the exhibits.

Sincerely,

Howard Brown
President

LK

Enclosure

Name: _____ Date: _____

Administrative Bodies

Directions: The business communications document below has several errors. Please proofread the document very carefully and correct all errors using the proper proofreader mark(s).

THE UNITED NATIONS STRUCTURE

1988

I. SECURITY COUNCIL: Fifteen members—the Big Five, permanent; ten elected for two-year terms by Assembly. Functions through:

    1. Atomic Energy Commission

    2. Military Staff Committee

    3. international contingents of armed forces

II. GENERAL ASSEMBLY: Member nations—159. Discusses questions relating to peace, security, and other matters under Charter; makes recommendations to Security Council; functions through these specialized agencies:

    1. Educational, scientific, and Cultural

    2. Food and Agriculture

    3. International labor

    4. International Civil aviation

    5. international Bank

    6. International Monetary Fund

    7. World Health

    8. International refugee

III. SECRETARIAL: Secretary-General at head; includes research, administrative staffs; reports to Security Council, Assembly.

IV. INTERNATIONAL COURT OF JUSTICE: Fifteen members chosen by the Assembly. Meets in permanent session to decide "judiciable" disputes that arise between nations.

Name: _____   Date: _____

Courses of Instruction

Directions: The business communications document below has several errors. Please proofread the document very carefully and correct all errors using the proper proofreader mark(s).

Patterson Free Academy
1605 Henderson Drive
Patterson, NJ 00000

Telephone 333 555-4467

March 22, 19--

Mrs. Elliott Green
246 Alto Vista Road
Waterloo, IA 50703

Dear Mrs. Green:

We shall be happy to welcome your daughter, Nancy, as one of our students when your family moves to Patterson. Since your daughter does not plan to attend college, we recommend that she enroll in our business education program. Stenographic training is an investment that can pay lifelong dividends to the person who does not want to be limited to a mediocre job. The demand for secretaries is so great that preparation in this area provides entry into every field of business and affords limitless opportunities for promotion. It is our sincere desire to perform a specific service for career-minded students.

Listed are some of the courses Nancy would be taking:

keyboarding	--1133
word processing	--4213
electronic communications	--2323
Desktop Publishing	--2533
electronic spreadsheets	--2632
Principles of Economics	--2013
principles of accounting	--2023

If you would like a copy of a booklet describing all the courses offerings of our business education department, mail the enclosed card.

Sincerely,

William Brownholtz
Program Director

MW

Enclosure

Name: _____   Date: _____

The Directions East, West, North, and South

Directions: The business communications document below has several errors. Please proofread the document very carefully and correct all errors using the proper proofreader mark(s).

Carson Travel Bureau
South Locust Street
Carson City, CA 90746   **Telephone 333 555-2332**

June 20, 19--

Miss Ester Norman
223 Johns Avenue
San Francisco, CA 94100

Dear Miss Norman:

Thank you very much for your enthusiastic letter of June 12. We were thrilled to learn of your interest in a trip to the far east and would be delighted to discuss it with you.

Our office is located on south Locust Street in nearby Carson City. We are situated in the very center of the street on the North side—you would turn left if you were facing the ocean.

We are enclosing some descriptive literature on some of the tours we are sponsoring this fall for you to inspect (before you visit our office) to get a general idea of some plans we can make for you. We are including, as you requested, plans not only for the far east but also for the middle east.

Please contact us soon so your holiday will be exactly as you wish it and you will have priority on the best accommodations—especially if you leave north America.

Sincerely yours,

Arthur Lesenberry
Manager

LDR

Enclosures

Name: _____ Date: _____

The Directions East, West, North, and South

Directions: The business communications document below has several errors. Please proofread the document very carefully and correct all errors using the proper proofreader mark(s).

June 17, 19--

Mr. Alexander Levin
197 north Fifty-fifth Street
Kingston, NH 03848

Dear Mr. Levin:

Thank you for answering our ad in the *Hornell Gazette.* I hope the following information will help you in your decision to purchase property in west Boston.

The town of Dennis offers "traditional" cape living. Three of the finest beaches in north America are located here. The Bass River forms the western boundary and has several marinas for boating enthusiasts. We are within easy access to medical facilities, since Boston is a short ten-minute drive East of us.

The cost of lots varies greatly, land near the water being more expensive. Waterfront lots range from $25,000 to $30,000. However, lots located in the areas designated on the enclosed map sell for less, since they are South of Dennis and are in a more heavily wooded area. These properties, though, are in beautiful year-round locations convenient to shopping, beaches, churches, and the Dennis golf course.

We have a fine selection of choice lots. Stop in and see us when you are in the area. Remember, the east is still a fine place to live.

Sincerely,

J. Walter White

RM

Enclosure

Name: _____ Date: _____

Typographical Errors

Directions: The business communications document below has several errors. Please proofread the document very carefully and correct all errors using the proper proofreader mark(s).

Ground Hill Road
New Paltz, NY 12560
November 29, 19--

Ms. Kavin Graham, Caseworker
Department of Social Services
Box 1800
Kingston, NY 12404

Dear Ms. Graham:

This is in reference to you letter of November 2, 19--, requesting information about the capabilties of Annette Corkey and Eric Adams as adoptive parents.

We have known Annette as a freind, nieghbor, and tenant for the past five years. We have found her to be reliable and dependable in every way. She is a very caring individual, most likly enhanced by her many years serving as a social worker.

We have known Eric for the past three years. Through his drive and determination, Eric has developed a highly successful and financialy sound landscape and plant maintenance business.

Eric and Annette were married two years ago and their relationship is a close one. The addition of Baby Tara to their lifes only completes the picture.

Eric and Annette are both well-educated and have a great love for nature. They are fine people who are financially, physically, and psychologically able to provide an excellent home for Tara.

Very truly yours,

Ron and Elizabeth Kramer

RI

Name: _____ Date: _____

Numbers

Directions: The business communications document below has several errors. Please proofread the document very carefully and correct all errors using the proper proofreader mark(s).

A C C O U N T I N G

A Rewarding Career

Accounting is one of the largest fields of professional employment, with almost a million people working in this occupation. It is also one of the highest-paying fields of work for which a young person can prepare.

A survey of more than 100 large business organizations shows that starting salaries average over $20,000 a year. Salaries of accountants with 10 years' experience are likely to be double or triple the beginning rate. Many accountants in supervisory positions or self-employed accountants earn between forty and sixty-five thousand dollars a year.

Accounting employment is expected to expand rapidly because of several factors: the general use of accounting information in an information society; business management; complex and changing tax systems; and the increasing use of accounting services by small business organizations.

Beginners in private accounting may start as ledger or cost clerks, timekeepers, junior internal auditors, or trainees for technical and executive positions. On the whole, accounting graduates are in greatest demand and are finding employment most often in small firms.

41

Name: _____   Date: _____

Paragraphs

Directions: The business communications document below has several errors. Please proofread the document very carefully and correct all errors using the proper proofreader mark(s).

TWENTIETH CENTURY, INC.
ONE ASSOCIATION LANE
PAOLI, OK 73074 _____

January 4, 19--

Miss Dorothy Greenleigh
2101 North Cedar Street
Paoli, OK 73074

Dear Miss Greenleigh:

The regular semiannual meeting of our General Policies Committee, of which you are a member, will be held in Delhi on Thursday and Friday, February 5 and 6. Kindly prepare a report covering the activities of your subcommittee since the date of our last meeting. Deliver two copies of your report to me and send one copy to each member of your subcommittee at least one week prior to the time of the meeting scheduled above. May I remind you that your expenses will be paid if you present vouchers with your expense account. The necessary reservation has been made for you at the Raleigh Hotel, headquarters for our meeting. If you have any matters that should be brought to the attention of Mr. George, please consult me about them before January 22.

Sincerely,

Clyde Anderson
General Manager

AW

Name: _____ Date: _____

Spelling

Directions: The business communications document below has several errors. Please proofread the document very carefully and correct all errors using the proper proofreader mark(s).

LOADING DOCK RESPONSIBILITIES

1. Whenever posible, outgoing plant shipments will take priority over incoming material.

2. When incoming supplies arrive at the plant, all efforts should be made to unload the trucks quickly in order to keep the bays open.

3. The gatekeper, who is in charge of all truck parking, will asign a number to all incoming trucks.

4. If all bays are ocupied when a truck arrives, the truck will be unloaded as soon as a bay is open and the truck's number is posted.

5. Since there may be times when several trucks are waiting, offloaded material may be stord on the docks in order to speed up unloading.

6. The dock superviser, who is in charge of all dock operations, will determine when material may be stored in the holding areas.

7. As soon as dock personal are available, the stored material will be delivered to the proper plant area.

8. The cheif foreman who is in charge of the specific section to which the material is being delivered must sign for all material.

9. Delivery slips that have been properly procesed must be returned to the dock supervisor by the end of each shift.

10. If there appears to be an error on the delivery slip, notify the dock supervisor imediately.

Name: _____ Date: _____

Spelling

Directions: The business communications document below has several errors. Please proofread the document very carefully and correct all errors using the proper proofreader mark(s).

BIKE SAFETY RULES

Biking is almost a year-round sport or means of transportation in most areas of the nation; only ice, snow, and/or biter cold will discourage bikers. Biking is good for fun and exercise; moreover, biking helps to save gasoline. Unfortunately, many thousands of people are seriously injured and some are killed each year in bike mishaps. A large share of the fatal accidents involve colisions with motor vehicles. Bike acidents can be prevented; in fact, a few timly reminders can help. For instance, when buying a bike be sure it is the corect size for the rider; be sure the rider can physicaly handle the bike. Not everyone needs a ten-sped racer. Second, be sure that the bike is mechanicaly sound and equipped with the proper lights, reflectors, and warning flag. Third, avoid horseplay and dangerous bike games. Fourth, be lawful—obey all trafic laws, signs, and signals; push your bike across busy intersections; always stay to the right; signal your intenshions when stopping and/or turning. Fifth, don't carry large items that could block your vision or make your bike difficult to handle. Because you have the right of way doesnt mean that you have to take it if theres doubt about the actions of a nearby motor vehicle; therefore, watch for cars pulling out into traffic lanes and for people opening car doors.

Name: _____ Date: _____

Spelling

Directions: The business communications document below has several errors. Please proofread the document very carefully and correct all errors using the proper proofreader mark(s).

GUIDE FOR SUCCESSFUL FISHING

1. Have you taken out your tackle and checked it to make sure everything you will need is their and in working condition? Unless your equipment is in good order, nothing else you do will make any difference.

2. Have you made plans for where you will fish? Since some spots are better than others, ask round and find out where fish activity is being reported.

3. Is your bate fresh and luring? After all is said and done, fresh bait catches fresh fish every time!

4. Do you have the proper clothes for where and when you are goin? Although clothes don't make the man or woman, being comfortible while you are fishing might make the trip more enjoyible.

5. Now you are ready. Don't forget to set the alarm! If you get an early start, you might get the early fish that are always out for their morning exercize. When the fish start biteing, remember to keep the big ones and throw the little ones back. Above all else, be careful!

Name: _____   Date: _____

Exercise 1

Directions: The business communications document below has several errors. Please proofread the document very carefully and correct all errors using the proper proofreader mark(s).

Lott-Shimmel Realty Company
One Realty Lane
Boulder, CO 80320

Telephone 333 555-6765

May 13 19--

Samuel Stevens
6 Larchment Drive
Boulder CO 80320

dear Mr. Stevens:

Lott-Shimmel Realty Co. sells more single-family dwellings in Colorado than any other real estate agency in the state. We have twenty-one offices located in the states bordering Colorado in adition to the sixteen here. We sold over $350 milion in residential property this past year. Lott-Shimmel Realty Co. opened its first office on March 4 1948.

Our staff is highly trained to serve you in your effort to buy a home with a veterans' administration (VA) loan. Our computer network alows you instant access to all available homes listed in our thirty-seven offices.

Since you expressed an interest at the home show in a possible move in the near future, we would be pleased to asist you in that decision. Our nearest office is located at 1200 Portland Place, in Boulder.

I would appreciate meeting with you at your earliest convenience. The summer months, traditionally the most active real estate season, are fast approaching and will afford the best chance for you to sell and buy. our office hours are listed on the enclosed card.

Sincerely

Ronald Kirshner
Broker

RI

Enclosure

Name: _____ Date: _____

Exercise 2

Directions: The business communications document below has several errors. Please proofread the document very carefully and correct all errors using the proper proofreader mark(s).

     TO: Bureau Counselors

  FROM: Peter Franzen, Manager

  DATE: June 18, 19--

SUBJECT; Tips on Buying a Used Car

We have had so many requests in the past month for assistance and informaion on buying and financing used cars that we have compiled a circular, Tips for Buying Used Cars, a copy of which is attached.

These circulars are now ready for use and distribution. However before this booklet goes in to permanent printing we would be interested in the reactions of your clients as to possible additons or changes.

Cleints who request this information should also be advised to compare costs of financing any loans before they commit themselves. commercial banks and credit unions sometimes charge less for loans than car dealers or the fanance companies through which they do business. Because charges vary according to geographic location, ask your clients to call on the credit department at their own bank or credit union?

JP

Name: _____ Date: _____

Exercise 3

Directions: The business communications document below has several errors. Please proofread the document very carefully and correct all errors using the proper proofreader mark(s).

> **Natural Pools & Spas, Inc.**
> **Box 600 State Street**
> **Terre Haute, Indiana 47811**
>
> **Telephone 333 555-9987**

March 8 19--

CUSTOMER NAME
STREET ADDRESS
CITY, STATE ZIP CODE

Dear (CUSTOMER NAME):

This letter and the enclosed "Spring Mailer" and Chemical Coupon sheet are being sent to you as a way of thanking you for doing business with us in the past.

With the '85 Swiming Season nearly upon us we invite you to take advantage of our unadvertised Specials in effect from April fourteen thru May thirteen. These prices are for you, our preferred customers, and they will not be advertised in the newspaper.

The Natural Pools & Spas Staff is continuing to grow, yet many of the familar faces remain. Warren Angermeye, our Production Coordinator, and Joseph Silas and Georgia Polishook, Salespeople, continue with us. Aditionally, our friendly office staffers Gerta Wallner and Amy Napolitano are now joined by Steven Porko.

We look forward to rewelcoming you to Natural Pools and Spas. When you visit, you will notice new products have been added to our ever-expanding lines: (Aqua Wash, Bacto-Kleen), and Sea-Chem as chemicals. In addition, our Waldo Sun-Room is on display adjacent to our showroom, and four new spa lines have been added to our collection.

We will be holding several "HOMEOWNERS' POOL CHEMISTRY SEMINARS." The first 1's will be Friday, may 11 at 7:00 P.M. and then Friday, June 1 at 7:00 P.M. and Saturday, june 2 at 10:00 A.M. and 2:00 P.M. Please plan to attend at least one seminar to refresh your "Water Chemistry." We're here to help!

Happy Swimming,

Art Newbury
President

Enclosure

RI

     Proofreading Practice

Name: _____ Date: _____

Exercise 4

Directions: The business communications document below has several errors. Please proofread the document very carefully and correct all errors using the proper proofreader mark(s).

GUIDE TO GOOD TRAVEL PICTURES

Before You Leave

Make sure your equipment is working properly. Check both your camera and flash to make sure the bateries are fresh. Since batteries deteriorate in certain weather conditions, be sure you have extras.

Take enough film. count on using at least one roll per day; two rolls, if taking movies? Carry the film with you when boarding the plane, as metal detectors used on luggage at some airports may cause exposure.

Snapping That Shutter

Watch for small details, and keep your pictures simple. Try to include a single idea. Be fore you snap your shutter check the edges of your viewfinder for distracting objects. Dont be afraid of your subject—move in close.

When photographing pople, keep them busy. Be sure to keep your horizon level. Try to include some foreground in panoramic scenes. REMEMBER TO HOLD THE CAMERA STEADY?

Have your film processed as soon as possible after it is exposed.

Name: _____   Date: _____

Exercise 5

Directions: The business communications document below has several errors. Please proofread the document very carefully and correct all errors using the proper proofreader mark(s).

TIPS ON BUYING A USED CAR

With some routine checks and a little mechanical know-how, you should be able to get your monies worth when you buy a used car. Shop around and compare prices, cars, and dealers. a dealer who sells new cars as well as used cars is usually well-equipped to stand behind his guarantee/

A. To help you evaluate the condition of the engine:

   1. Test the engine when it is cold. if blue smoke comes from the exhaust, it could mean the engine is burning oil and neds repairs.

   2. start from a slow speed and accelerate rapidly. If the engine jerks or balks, something may be wrong?

B. To help you know if the car has been in an accident

   1. Look for signs of dents and wrinkles.

   2. Check both sides of the radiator for repair work.

C. To help you estimate the true milage:

   1. Notice the condition and brand of the tires.

   2. Check the rubber of the brake pedal. It wears thin after twenty thousand miles.

     Proofreading Practice